Ex Líbrís

Plate 1. Edward Sackville, 4th Earl of Dorset, by William Larkin, 1613.
The Suffolk Collection, Rangers House, Blackheath (Greater London Council).

AN ILLUSTRATED GUIDE

TO

LACE

Emily Reigate

Antique Collectors' Club

First published 1986
© Emily Reigate 1986
World copyright reserved

Reprinted 1988, 1996

ISBN 1 85149 003 5

British Library Cataloguing-in-Publication Data
A catalogue record for this book is available from the British Library

Printed in England on Consort Royal Satin from Donside Mills, Aberdeen,
by the Antique Collectors' Club, Woodbridge, Suffolk, IP12 1DS

Antique Collectors' Club

The Antique Collectors' Club was formed in 1966 and quickly grew to a five figure membership spread throughout the world. It publishes the only independently run monthly antiques magazine, *Antique Collecting*, which caters for those collectors who are interested in widening their knowledge of antiques, both by greater awareness of quality and by discussion of the factors which influence the price that is likely to be asked. The Antique Collectors' Club pioneered the provision of information on prices for collectors and the magazine still leads in the provision of detailed articles on a variety of subjects.

It was in response to the enormous demand for information on 'what to pay' that the price guide series was introduced in 1968 with the first edition of *The Price Guide to Antique Furniture* (completely revised 1978 and 1989), a book which broke new ground by illustrating the more common types of antique furniture, the sort that collectors could buy in shops and at auctions rather than the rare museum pieces which had previously been used (and still to a large extent are used) to make up the limited amount of illustrations in books published by commercial publishers. Many other price guides have followed, all copiously illustrated, and greatly appreciated by collectors for the valuable information they contain, quite apart from prices. The Price Guide Series heralded the publication of many standard works of reference on art and antiques. *The Dictionary of British Art* (now in six volumes), *Oak Furniture* and *Early English Clocks* were followed by many deeply researched reference works such as *The Directory of Gold and Silversmiths*, providing new information. Many of these books are now accepted as the standard work of reference on their subject.

The Antique Collectors' Club has widened its list to include books on gardens and architecture. All the Club's publications are available through bookshops world wide and a full catalogue of all these titles is available free of charge from the addresses below.

Club membership, open to all collectors, costs little. Members receive free of charge *Antique Collecting*, the Club's magazine (published ten times a year), which contains well-illustrated articles dealing with the practical aspects of collecting not normally dealt with by magazines. Prices, features of value, investment potential, fakes and forgeries are all given prominence in the magazine.

Among other facilities available to members are private buying and selling facilities, the longest list of 'For Sales' of any antiques magazine, an annual ceramics conference and the opportunity to meet other collectors at their local antique collectors' clubs. There are over eighty in Britain and more than a dozen overseas. Members may also buy the Club's publications at special pre-publication prices.

As its motto implies, the Club is an organisation designed to help collectors get the most out of their hobby: it is informal and friendly and gives enormous enjoyment to all concerned.

For Collectors — By Collectors — About Collecting

ANTIQUE COLLECTORS' CLUB
5 Church Street, Woodbridge Suffolk IP12 1DS, UK
Tel: 01394 385501 Fax: 01394 384434
—— or ——
Market Street Industrial Park, Wappingers' Falls, NY 12590, USA
Tel: 914 297 0003 Fax: 914 297 0068

Acknowledgements

I owe a great deal to a great many people and I would particularly like to thank the following:

Ann Collier	Marie Jarkouska
Mo Gibbs	The Lace Guild
B. Hanujova	Isobel Rendell
	Sandra C. Straughair

for allowing me to use their copyright designs as illustrations.

Mrs. Rachel Gouldsmith   Mrs. Margery Watson
Mrs. Bettina Warren

for allowing me to use photographs of interesting lace which they own.

Miss Jean Mailey   Mrs. Gunnel Teitel
Miss Margaret Nolan

for showing me the collection, and helping me to find and use illustrations of lace at the Metropolitan Museum of Art.

Miss Santina Levey and Judy Wentworth for helping me to learn about lace.

Mr. Wright of the Photographic Department at Harrods for helping me with photographic techniques.

Lorna MacEchern, Secretary to the Duke of Buccleuch and Queensberry, for her help in finding a portrait.

Mrs. Alison Riley, for endless, no doubt boring, typing.

Notes

Dating: In this book specific dates are used wherever possible. All dating is to some extent guesswork, and one must allow ten years on either side of each date given, but specific dates make one think clearly and are therefore more likely to be accurate.

Measurements: Feet and inches were used all over Europe until Napoleon introduced the metric system. The lace in this book has therefore been measured in inches.

To John

Colour Plates

Contents

Lace-making Centres

CHAPTER I

An Introduction to
Lace Making and Collecting

Lace is an unusual textile in that it was made wholly in Europe. There was no lace in China or Peru, or in India or Japan. It is a purely European invention. The technique was carried by missionaries to other lands, but there little original work was done. We need not, then, look beyond Europe (see map opposite).

The other peculiarity about lace is that it was made by the poorest women and worn by the richest men and women in Europe. In the seventeenth and eighteenth centuries, fine lace cost more than jewels and was guarded and prized accordingly. The making of lace was organized in different ways in different places. Basically what was needed was an efficient person with enough money to pay for the costly thread, an accurate sense of fashion to choose the right designs, and the toughness to drive the unfortunate workers. In some cases, lace making was organized by convents or beguinages (Belgian almshouses), in others by lace masters or mistresses or, rarely, by the head of a large household. Bells to summon servants were not used until late in the eighteenth century, and many a poor relation spent her time waiting to be sent on errands. While waiting, she could sew, mend, embroider or make lace.

Lace in the seventeenth, eighteenth and nineteenth centuries could be compared with the automobile of the twentieth century, in that neither can be truthfully described as a necessity, but everyone wants to own the best he can afford. There was constant appreciation and rivalry. The same comparison can be made in the economic field. Governments could not cope, in the seventeenth century, with money going overseas for lace, as today they worry about the import of Japanese cars.

The first reference we have to lace is in a will made by one of the ruling Milanese Sforza family in 1493. Many pattern books and directions for making lace were printed in the first half of the sixteenth century; but very few were printed after about 1565. We must assume, therefore, that after that date lace was no longer made as a hobby, but had become commercialised. However, it is clear that for another century at least lace was made at home in England. Quite a lot of early needle lace of great charm and elaboration with English looking flowers can be found.

Lace was worn at all levels of society, and as the doctor's wife could obviously not afford the lace made for a princess, lace of different qualities was made.

The quality of lace depends on the quality of the thread and the skill of the workers. The thread was so very expensive that it was sensible only to supply it to the best workers. The designs were less important because lace

This amusing picture shows women making lace a hundred and twenty-five years ago. The same methods are used today. However, nowadays lace is made for fun.
Illustration from *History of Lace* by Mrs. Bury Palliser, Plate XVIII.

was almost always gathered or frilled, or worn with the fulness pushed together, as the end of a scarf. The cap back was the only piece of lace worn virtually flat, just slightly curved to fit the back of the head, and, with dark hair behind it, one could clearly see the design. Why women wore caps for centuries is a question to which there seems no answer. Mediaeval women wore swooping caps, women of the 1870s wore plain caps with lace frills, and everything possible in shape was worn in between. Perhaps with rough soap and no easy hot water, women washed their hair rarely, and found themselves going bald at an early age. But in the 1880s, there were ladies' maids who were expected to brush the hair for half an hour each evening. That must have meant fine thick hair for the younger woman, and perhaps that is why only older women wore caps.

The design of lace was, of course, linked to the designs of other crafts. When the European fashion was for Chinese blue and white china in the 1730s and '40s, there were chinoiserie designs on lace. Pillement, 1727-1808, designed for porcelain and printed textiles and his designs were engraved. We do not know that he designed for lace, but any good technician designing for lace would have been able to adapt his designs. Again, when classical ideas began to come in during the 1760s, the lace designers did their best. As almost all lace borders were worn ruffled, the design did not really show. Only the wide pieces designed to be worn stitched flat on dresses of the 1760s and '70s properly displayed their designs. These pieces were made with double edges and are particularly beautiful and sought after. Lappets can be very lovely, but judging from portraits, they were rarely worn plainly so that their design showed. All too often they were tied with bows, or folded on top of the head. Presumably they were only worn on special occasions, since although so few are shown, many thousands of them exist. The cap backs, lappets and borders for trimming the dress were supposed to match. We rarely see portraits where this can be truthfully said to be so.

In the nineteenth century, a great deal of lace was worn. Much of it was either old or copied from old lace. This was the lace most highly prized. The beautiful shawls which did not imitate earlier designs, were also appreciated, but most of 'Grandma's lace' is nostalgic. Without the fine thread, it was impossible to copy old lace exactly, but the magnificent natural flowers on the shawls which did not copy old designs are wonderful and should, one feels, be more appreciated today.

HISTORY

In the sixteenth century lace was used to join together pieces of linen, to make sheets decorative, for instance. It was also used to decorate altar cloths and other church linens. The very fine spidery narrow borders would have been used on ruffs. Many ruffs had elaborately embroidered borders, and to be able to buy lace instead must have been a blessing.

In the seventeenth century lace became heavier as the ruff was abandoned and falling collars came in. These were followed in the middle of the century with scarves and kerchiefs, ended or bordered with lace. The Princes of the Church used a great deal of lace. Their albs were trimmed with wide lace borders and matching cuffs, and whole altar frontals in lace were made in large numbers. It is astonishing how much lace of this period still survives. There are enormous quantities of Milanese lace of every width to be found in every auction room where lace is sold. Much of it is run of the mill stuff with dreary uninteresting designs, but it is marvellous how long it has lasted.

In the eighteenth century, lace became much lighter, partly for reasons of fashion, because it could be ruffled, and partly for reasons of economy because so much more could be made from a pound of thread. These elegant light laces with contemporary designs are very beautiful; the heavier Italian laces disappeared from view. At the end of the century, neo-classical fashions did not need lace. Also, the first machine-made net appeared in 1763. The combination of these factors destroyed the lace market for thirty or forty years.

By the beginning of the nineteenth century, little lace was made by hand. A market for machine-made laces gradually developed, but in the 1830s many of the rich demanded expensive handmade lace. These laces were made in a few centres like Brussels and Chantilly, and in any way that fashion demanded. Valenciennes, for example, was made all over Northern France. The names became generic and no longer represented places. Lace was much used in dress and for large articles like shawls or curtains. This meant that all sorts of new techniques were developed. At the same time, many charitable ladies were starting lace schools to help the poor, from

Ireland to Venice. In most cases, these schools produced fine quality lace to excellent designs.

Enormous quantities of nineteenth century lace appear at every lace sale. Many many people own boxes of 'Grandma's lace'. Seventy-five per cent of this lace is nineteenth century. It is light and pretty and should give pleasure to those who wear it. The early twentieth century brought a resurgence of interest in, what was then called, 'real' lace. Occasionally one finds a very beautiful piece of twentieth century lace, showing art nouveau influence.

In the twentieth century, lace totally vanished from dress, thanks to Paul Poiret who transformed women's dress in the period immediately before the First World War, designing clothes which followed the shape of the body, and were no longer dependent on corsets and padding. Some lace curtains were still made by machine and so was wide lace from which dresses could be made. The designs leave much to be desired. At the moment there are many thousands of women making lace as a hobby. They are very enthusiastic and it is to be hoped that their interest will long continue.

FASHION

Fashion and lace are hopelessly entwined. When lace technique moved forward, fashion used the improved fabric. When fashion changed, lace had to be made to fit it. It's the usual question of the chicken and the egg. The first lace books of the 1550s and '60s show patterns for their spidery laces. The pointed ones were obviously meant for ruffs. Expensive ruffs were made of elaborately embroidered, very fine cloth. To be able to add a lace edge and not to have to embroider it, must have made a big difference to the time needed and therefore to the cost. These delicate edgings were copied in coarser thread and used on things like altar cloths and household linen. The straight edged bobbin laces often had needle lace scalloped edgings added, and the reverse was true with bobbin scallops added to needle lace straight pieces.

Ruffs were introduced in 1540 when Henri IV of France wanted something made to cover a scar on his neck, and they were worn for half a century. The idea of a ruff obviously appealed to the people of the time, as did the high starched lace collars of the first twenty years of the seventeenth century. The starched collars show off a head as a ruff did. Ruffs and high collars must have been very uncomfortable to wear. At home, en famille, soft turning collars must have been worn for comfort. This is the sort of collar shown in the portrait of Lord Southampton (plate 3, opposite). He was imprisoned in the Tower for the years 1600-03, and he had no need to wear anything uncomfortable. He is shown wearing a plain collar trimmed with a pointed edge, presumably a piece of lace made for a ruff thirty years before. His cuffs, on the other hand, are very smart with their black bows. He was doing his best under difficult conditions, one feels. Lord Dorset's lace on his collar and cuffs do match (frontispiece). This portrait of 1613 shows a man dressed in the height of fashion. He has black lace around his knees and red lace pompons on his shoes. Lace was really appreciated in those days. We know nothing of English lace at that time, and so we must assume that this was all Flemish lace.

The Dutch woman painted by Frans Hals in 1630 (plate 4, page 17) is also

Plate 2. *Sir Walter Raleigh, 1552-1618. Miniature by Hilliard, 1585. Raleigh is dressed after the Italian fashion. The lace edge of his ruff is quite clear, though one cannot see if it is bobbin or needle made. The curious look of the head resting on a platter seems to have been much admired. Even when ruffs were given up, the high collars, as shown in the portrait of Lord Dorset (frontispiece), still have the same effect.*

By courtesy of the National Portrait Gallery, London.

Plate 3. *Henry, 3rd Earl of Southampton, by John de Critz the elder, 1555-1642. This portrait was painted between 1600 and 1603 while the Earl was in the Tower of London. The lace on his collar was the type made for the trimming of an ordinary ruff thirty years before.*

In the collection of the Duke of Buccleuch and Queensberry K.T., at Boughton House, Kettering, England.

wearing a complicated starched collar, edged with the best quality white Flemish lace. It is interesting that the lace on her collar and cuffs and the lace of her bonnet do not match.

The picture of Lord and Lady Capel and their five children of twenty five years later (plate 5, opposite below) shows the total change in fashion. The wide scalloped borders on the collars of the adults and around the necklines of the little girls are echoed in the narrow laces of the cuffs. Again the laces do not match. The baby wears a cap, but Lady Capel and her daughters are wearing coloured ribbons in their hair. The importance of lace for display is clear in this picture. The scalloped lace is soft and white and has been made for this use.

After this date, many thousands of portraits show lace, but it is very difficult to see exactly what it is, although these pictures were painted at a time when meticulous attention to detail was all important, so we know we are seeing what the painter saw. The adaptation of lace to fashion is clear, and we can assume that the same sort of thing went on continually.

'Drizzling', the removal of silver and gold from thread, became a fashionable pastime during the last twenty years of the eighteenth century. The best furniture makers of the day made beautiful gadgets of mahogany and brass for this purpose. Two wheels revolved when a handle was turned and old threads dropped into one box and silver or gold into the other. In this way the gold and silver braids and lace of Europe were almost totally destroyed during the twenty or thirty years the fashion lasted. It is difficult for us to imagine the destruction. We don't think of eighteenth century dress as glittering with gold, but in fact it probably did. We know that the Stuart Court did from many descriptions. King Charles brought the fashion here from France, and so it was commented on, but by the eighteenth century it was totally accepted. Now it is rare indeed to see a piece of gold or silver lace; occasionally one sees a gold epaulette in a museum, but even that is uncommon.

DESIGN

In Flanders the guilds had always controlled wool weaving and other textile making. When lace became big business early in the seventeenth century, it was immediately controlled in the same way. This had certain advantages; the standards of design and technique were high and quality was insisted on. In Venice and Genoa, the city authorities also insisted on standards. The difficulties lay in the countryside around the towns. There the guilds did not hold sway in the same way, and poor quality lace was made in large quantities. The furnishing lace called Brabant is an example of this. So are the poor laces connected with Burano. Today the lace dealers in Burano proudly show one second rate Venetian lace and boast of its having been made in Burano. Presumably in both cases, the makers could not afford the best thread and that is why the lace seems loose and floppy, although the designs are often fine.

The design of any textile must be what the public wants. Public taste moves slowly but inexorably and not even the best French designer in modern times can persuade women to wear long skirts if they want to wear

Plate 4. Portrait of a woman, by Frans Hals, 1580-1666. The fine soft white Flemish lace is very beautiful. The bow on her bodice looks as if it might have been made of silver lace. The lace on her cap is narrow and dentate.
Reproduced by courtesy of the Trustees, The National Gallery, London.

Plate 5. The 1st Baron Capel and his family, by C. Johnson, 1639. This lace is worn in the same way as in the Frans Hals portrait above. Fashion was very similar all over Europe.
By courtesy of the National Portrait Gallery, London.

short ones. To design for lace was even more difficult as it took so long for a piece of lace to be made. When in about 1690-1700, dress became simpler and soft delicate lace that ruffled well was wanted, it took the various lace centres years to adjust. Venice never succeeded and lost its standing in the lace world. France took several years and may have tried various directions such as point de Sedan, before producing the very light delicate Alençon. Brussels, on the other hand, was ready for the challenge. The fine muslin being worn as caps, collars and cuffs was quickly supplanted by bobbin lace, solid looking, but with enchantingly natural leaves and flowers. Mechlin,

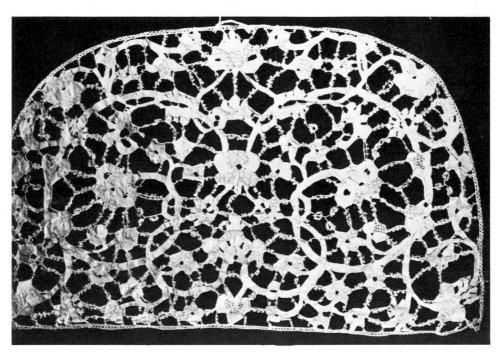

England, 1650 or earlier. This cap back looks to the scroll shapes of the renaissance for its inspiration. It has been lovingly worked with natural looking flowers, a pansy and pinks, and birds, all linked with elaborate bars. The thread is white and the cap back large. All this points to its being a piece of English lace, made with pleasure by an amateur. There have always been fine needlewomen in England and this piece of lace is in that tradition. The design fits well into the space; it is accomplished and pleasing, but perhaps a little thin.

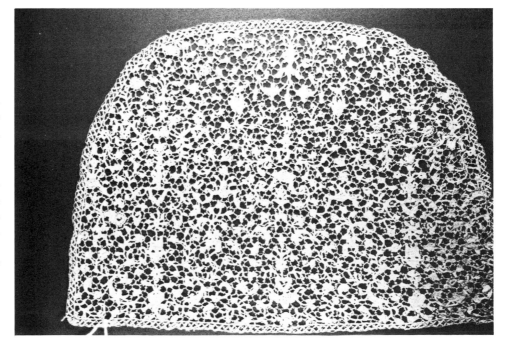

Venice, 1690. This cap back shows the poor design which caused Venice to lose the lead in the lace business. It is a rather pointless, boring design, and even the individual units do not have interesting shapes. Venetian teachers were imported into France to teach lace making. To tell the difference between early French and Venetian lace, look at the picots under a good lens. The Venetian picots have tiny knots or knobs, the French picots are smooth. The difference in technique is clear.

Valenciennes and the rest quickly followed suit. The day of bobbin lace had come and needle lace was fighting to stay in demand. Lace was generally used as a ruffle. The only shape of lace that was meant to be worn flat and which was worn for a long period was the cap back. It is interesting to see how the odd shape was filled by the design and how slowly the designs changed over the years. The designs reflect those used for brocaded textiles as well as the designs engraved on silver or painted on porcelain. Designers in any medium unconsciously absorb the ideas around them and interpret them in their work.

Brussels, 1700. Point d'Angleterre. The very fine thread used for this cap back gives it the lightness and feel of muslin. Through a lens, the solid pieces are seen to be all woven, and appear to be cloth. The palm tree was a religious symbol connected with the Holy Land. By 1700 it had lost some of its religious connotation. The design is beautifully planned to fill the space.

Mechlin, 1710. This is a large cap back, 12ins. across at the base; it does not lie flat. The elegant design is symmetrical and rich, with a truly baroque flavour. The border might be described as rococo with its asymmetrical shield design similar to those engraved on contemporary silver coffee or teapots.

19

Plate 6. Five children of Charles I, 1637. Painting after Van Dyck. The royal children wore a great deal of lace. It is interesting to compare the quality with that of the lace worn by the family group, opposite page.
By courtesy of the National Portrait Gallery, London.

Plate 7. James II, 1633-1701. Painting by an unknown artist, c.1690. The King is wearing a splendid piece of lace which appears to date from about 1650.
By courtesy of the National Portrait Gallery, London.

Plate 8. A family group, by Gonzales Coques, 1614 or
1618-1684. From the lace it can be estimated that the picture was
painted about 1660. It shows the quantity of lace worn by people
at that time. The lace is straight, being later than the scalloped
royal lace shown opposite.
Reproduced by courtesy of the Trustees, The National Gallery,
London.

Plate 9. Prince James Francis Stuart, 1688-1766, and his sister,
by Nicholas de Largillière. This picture which must have been
painted about 1695, shows the Princess's fashionable high head-
dress. Her apron and the Prince's cravat and cuffs are very fine.
By courtesy of the National Portrait Gallery, London.

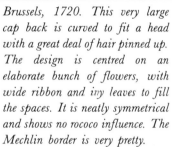

Brussels, 1720. This very large cap back is curved to fit a head with a great deal of hair pinned up. The design is centred on an elaborate bunch of flowers, with wide ribbon and ivy leaves to fill the spaces. It is neatly symmetrical and shows no rococo influence. The Mechlin border is very pretty.

Above right: Brussels, 1730. The design enclosing the central flowers has a much more definite shape. The palm trees at the sides have their top leaves formed by characteristic Brussels lines of loops.

England, Honiton, 1740. The shaped centre panels are now the most important feature of the design; the outer panels subordinate. This is a beautiful piece of lace with lovely English flowers well designed. Honiton lace was very popular in France during the 18th century. The sale of this lace alone brought in the equivalent of a million pounds annually in today's money from France.

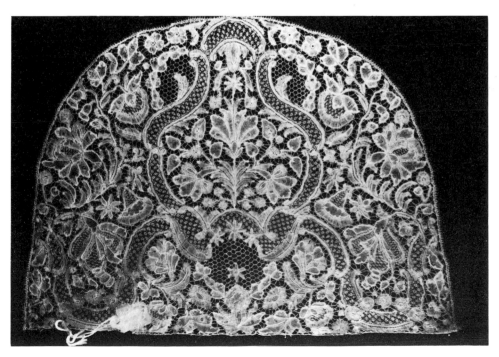

France, Alençon, 1740. Again the centre panel is all important, and the working of the pattern is crisp. It is interesting to compare this with the preceding bobbin lace cap back. The spotted sections in both examples give tonality to the design.

Left: France, Argentan, 1750. This cap back shows the same superb technique but the ground is more evident and the design lighter. The marvellous crispness of needle lace can be seen here.

Below: Brussels, 1750. Here the design is even lighter but the central shape still dominates.

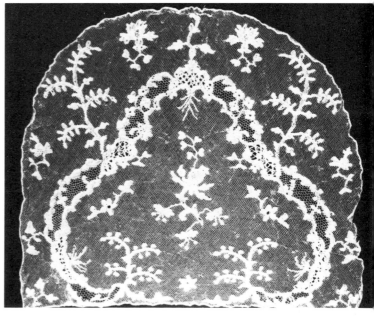

Plate 10. Angela Georgina, Baroness Burdett Coutts, 1814-1906, by W.C. Ross. She is wearing a handsome lace bertha and carrying a lace shawl.
By courtesy of the National Portrait Gallery, London.

France, Argentan, 1760. Needle lace cap back with matching lappet. The centre panel is still in place; the flowers are lighter and bear little resemblance to nature. The border matches that on the lappet and the flowers are alike.

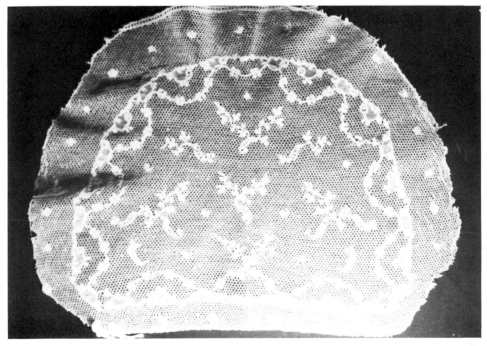

Argentan, 1770. The solid Argentan ground is still to be seen. Oddly enough, this ground does not wear well, and Argentan pieces are often found re-mounted onto net, or replaced by an Alençon ground. This odd looking cap back has not had a border added to it, but was made like this. Presumably it has never been made up into a cap and has never been worn.

TECHNIQUES

There are two basic ways of making lace: needle lace is made with a needle and thread using buttonhole stitch, and bobbin lace is made by twisting threads around the pins which determine the pattern.

Needle lace. There are many different ways of making a buttonhole stitch, but the net result is a hard wearing, rather rough surface. The flat areas of the design are ridged. It is slow to make, and was probably made by different people with the complicated bits of design being worked by the most experienced hand and the joining together being done by a less good worker. The design was drawn onto a piece of vellum and then it was placed onto a pillow. The outlines were sewn first and the fillings then put in. To make a long piece, the lace was removed to one end and the design repeated. The piece of design was called the repeat. Repeats vary in length from four inches or less to twenty-two inches or more. The pillow had, of course, to be a suitable size. The size of repeats does not have any bearing on the date or place of manufacture of the lace.

Buttonhole stitch is essentially a loop with a half caught knot. There are many different kinds of knots and many, many sorts of buttonhole stitch. In some the loop is more important than the knot and in others complicated knots are laid closely together. Some kinds of needle lace are worked from the back, such as hollie point, and others are worked from the front, such as gros point de Venise. The variation is enormous. The easiest way to differentiate between needle lace and bobbin lace is by the solids. It is almost impossible to plain weave with a single needle and thread and so the solid pieces of the design in needle lace are made of rows of knots and are not woven. There is a logical development in the discovery of needle made lace which cannot be proven, but which seems certain.

First came the wish to decorate a hem. This could be done by embroidery. A pattern of stitches could be made. Then by using a fine thread and pulling regularly a line of holes would appear. To make the holes bigger, one or more threads could be withdrawn, thus making hem stitching. Finally whole squares of thread could be cut out and replaced by diagonals; the edges and introduced threads would be buttonholed so that they would be strong enough to withstand washing and ironing. The final step would be lace itself: threads laid in a pattern, solid pieces buttonhole stitched and finally the solid pieces joined by bars. Curves soon appeared and the right angles from a woven fabric could be forgotten. The various stages are called pulled fabric work, pulled thread work, cut work, reticella (an embroidered needle lace made in a framework of squares), and punto in aria (a lace which has no ground).

Needle lace has always been regarded as finer than bobbin lace as it takes longer to make and therefore is more expensive. The elaborate bars of seventeenth century lace were copied in bobbin lace, but they never have its crispness. The design for a piece of needle lace was drawn out on a piece of vellum or paper. This was mounted onto a piece of linen on a pillow. This pillow, when placed on the knee, made the work easy to see. Threads were stretched along the edges and tacked around the design. The design was then worked. The bars were made to hold the toile together, and the whole was then cut free and the vellum used again.

Once lace makers had discovered that there was no need for right angles they quickly started making what we call lace. The design books of the 1550s and '60s show hundreds of designs for bobbin lace and embroidery and these could of course be copied by needle lace makers.

From the beginning needle lace makers invented different stitches. Lace developed as an airy fabric extraordinarily quickly. The early black and white squared designs, as in Buratto, soon acquired lights and shades from the use of different stitches. It is well worthwhile using a magnifying glass and getting to know the different stitches used.

The designers for needle lace used the new stitches to make lace of unparalleled beauty. In the seventeenth century the lace makers were paid so little, and the rich were so very rich that no one minded how long it took to make a piece of lace. The result was lace made with a wide variety of stitches. These can be seen in the following illustrations.

Italy, 1570. The small holes are made by pulled fabric work; the square holes are cut work with needle lace fillings. Width 1½ins.

Flanders, 1575. This is a true lace with buttonholed threads, based on right angle threads and roundels on top. Width 1½ins.

27

Italy or Flanders, 1580. A handsome mixture of roundels and diagonal lines, making a strong design. Width 3½ ins.

Italy or Flanders, 1590. The half roundels and hen filling show more freedom from rectangles. Note the tassels on the ends of the points. Width 5½ ins.

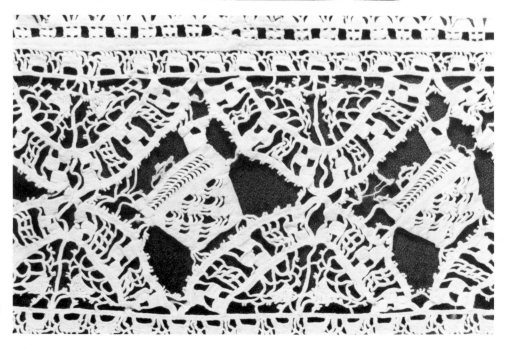

Detail showing the wonderful workmanship.

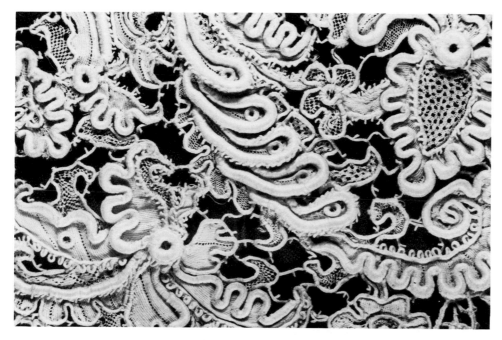

Point d'Espagne, probably made at Venice, 1660. Note the fineness of the thread and the knots on the end of the picots. The 'worms' of solid thread identify this as point d'Espagne.

France, Argentan, 1680. The ribbed solids are clear. Note the French smooth picots on the bars.

France, Argentan, 1740. Cap back. Again, the rough ribbed solids in the design are clear.

Bobbin lace can be made in three ways. *Straight lace* is the lace made from beginning to end with the same number of threads. None are added or subtracted. This obviously requires a lot of care on the part of the designer and the whole piece must be made by the same person as everyone works with a different tension. Again, the design was drawn on vellum and placed on a pillow. But for this lace pins are placed upright on the design and the thread knotted or twisted around them. The flat part of the design looks woven and cannot be mistaken for needle lace.

Part lace is worked by different people. The motifs are made separately and are then joined together, whether by bar or mesh ground.

Mixed lace is a mixture of needle and bobbin laces. Sometimes needle made motifs are joined by mesh worked by bobbins or more usually the motifs are applied to net, sometimes handmade, frequently machine-made. Mixed lace is a good example of cheapening the cost of lace making.

The seventeenth century was the century of needle lace, but the bobbin lace makers used their eyes and did their best to follow the needle lace designs and techniques. Bobbin lace makers started by copying or trying to copy needle lace stitches but soon invented dozens of stitches to give different tones. Some of these stitches were so slow to make that they were dropped when they made the lace too expensive and the wide range of stitches used in, for instance, early Milanese lace, soon became only one or two in the later lace. A number of different stitches are shown in the following pages. Some of the stitches became the grounds of lace at a later date. In the middle of the eighteenth century, many laces could be definitely named by their grounds. When lace re-emerged in 1820-30, lace making was so widespread that the names refer to a kind of lace and no longer to the place where it was made.

A pricking, showing how the holes made to hold the pins marked out the design. The upright pins held the threads as they were twisted, thus leaving the holes in the lace. Victoria and Albert Museum.

The designs for bobbin lace were also drawn on vellum and the vellum then placed onto a pillow, but that was all that the two methods had in common. The designs in bobbin lace were pricked with pins which stood up in the pillow. The threads were then twisted about the pins leaving holes where the pins had been. To make a strip, the piece of lace was moved along and the design repeated. In the late sixteenth century, the idea of making a strip, by moving the lace along, was not fully understood — some early Milan lace was made in pieces and then the rectangles were sewn together. In a lace like Valenciennes, where the fabric was worked straight across, the designs had to be well thought out. The hundreds of threads had to be carried through the toile and the ground without being cut or added to. In less fine lace, threads were cut and added, which often helps in the identification of the lace. In Flanders the lace of the seventeenth and eighteenth centuries, where the design was made first, and the ground added later, the threads of the ground can be found looped across the back of the toile in thin rope. These looped threads were sometimes used on the front as a cordonnet to give weight to one side of a bit of design, like a leaf. Brussels lace was made by many different hands with a specialist making each bit. These pieces were finally put together and finished by the most important specialist of all.

Italy, very close to a pattern in Le Pompe, a book of patterns for Venetian lace published in 1559. Width 1in.

Flanders, early 17th century. Collar, needle lace with bobbin border. Width 1¾ins.

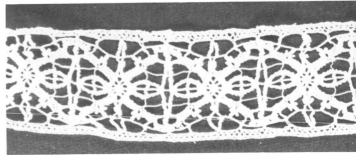

Applied lace*.* This method of lace making made the lace cheaper. In the eighteenth century, for instance, Alençon sent needlemade motifs to Brussels to be applied to handmade Brussels bobbin ground. After 1763 when machine-made net became commercially available, a great deal of needle and bobbin lace was applied to it. Machine net was also much used as a basis for embroidery, either by needle or with a tiny hook, worked on a frame, hence the name tambour lace. This last type of lace was much used in the 1820s and '30s after Heathcoat had invented his machine that made a diamond shaped ground, not square, but not round either!

This lace, too, is very close to a pattern in Le Pompe. Width 1½ins.

GROUNDS

Grounds seem an obviously easy way to sort lace. The trouble is that in many cases each specific ground was only used for a comparatively short time. Grounds can first be found as filling stitches when bars were used. Bars became more numerous in order to lighten the lace and to save money. For the first half of the eighteenth century, grounds were used consistently in bobbin lace in several places. But other fancier grounds were often used in all these places, and so the other characteristics of each lace need to be studied, appreciated and remembered. The laces of those fifty years are distinct, though their designs are much alike. Fashion was obviously all important to a textile industry like lace and the different lace masters must have watched their competitors like hawks.

a. Alençon, needle.

b. Argentan, needle.

c. Brussels, bobbin.

d. Mechlin, bobbin.

e. Round Valenciennes.

f. Square Valenciennes.

g. Lille, bobbin.

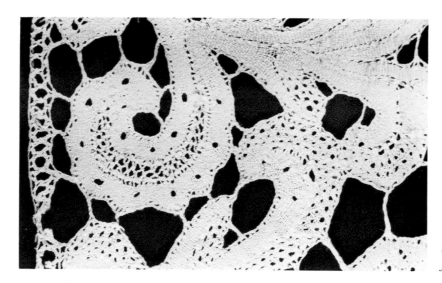

Genoa, 1700. Plain bars, whole stitch solid sections with different filling stitches.

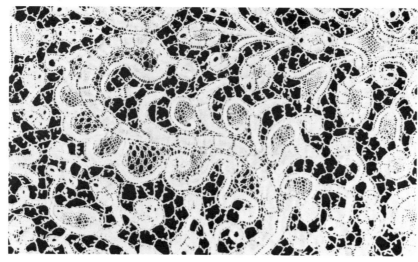

Flanders, 1700. Picoted bars, with many elaborate filling stitches. Note half stitch, cinq trous and kat stitch.

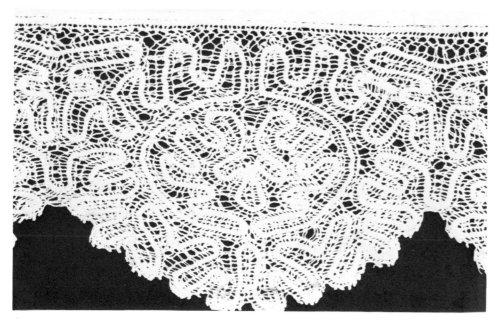

Flanders, 1630. Bars which are turning into mesh. Width 4ins.

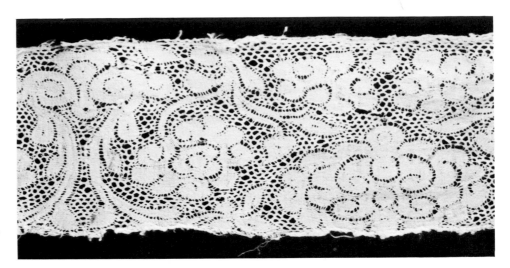

Flanders, 1630. An uneven and tentative round ground.

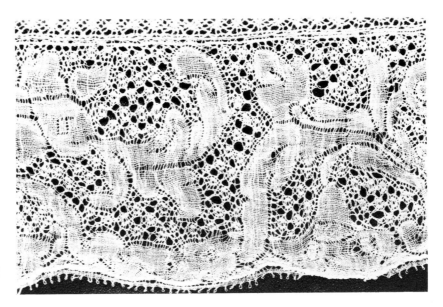

Binche, 1690. A snowball ground — one of many variations.

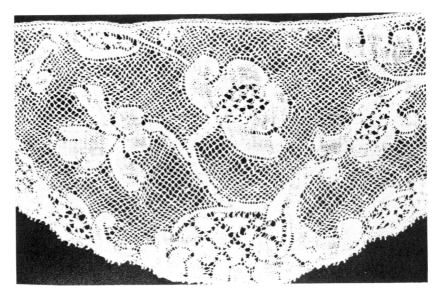

Flanders, 1690. Torchon, a very simple, much used ground. Width 4ins.

Flanders, 1700. A round ground worked every which way.

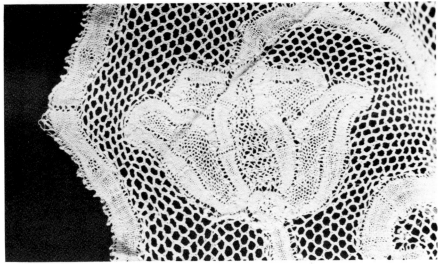

Detail showing the round ground twisting about the design. The centre petal is barred, the side petals half stitch.

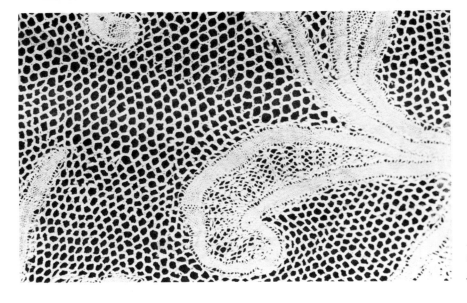

Detail showing barred stitches used to shape a leaf. The plaited round ground shows clearly.

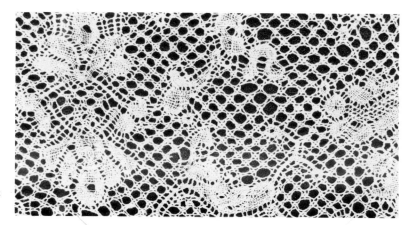

Binche, 1700. An early piece with an irregular cinq trous ground.

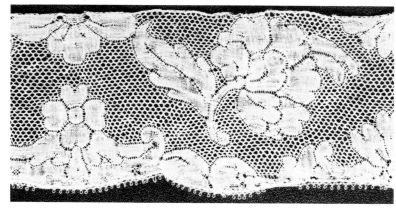

Valenciennes, 1730. A regular round ground. The neat, holed edges of the motifs are characteristic of Binche and Valenciennes.

Right: Mechlin, 1700. Fond de neige and cinq trous ground. Width 1½ins.

Below: Mechlin, 1700. Fond d'armure ground, a variation of the more usual solid ball centre.

Below right: Mechlin, 1730. Cinq trous ground; each worked rectangle looks like the five of hearts. A ground much used, and in many places. Width 2ins.

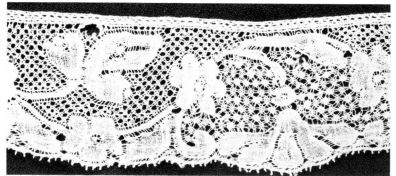

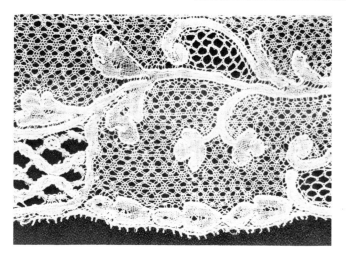

England, 1780. Kat stitch was widely used as a ground. Width 2½ins.

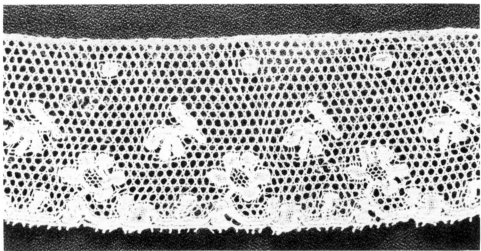

Mechlin, 1790. Kat stitch again. Width 1¾ins.

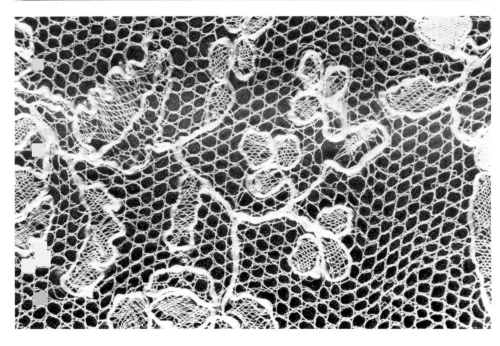

England, 1830. A scarf of blonde with a very fine silk kat stitch ground.

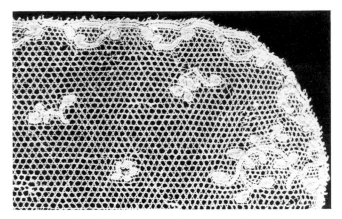

Point de Paris, 1860. Lappet with a kat ground, made as a copy of an 18th century design.

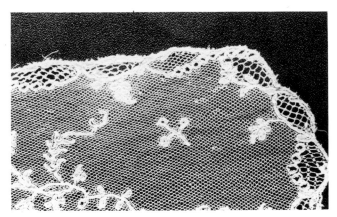

Mechlin, 1780. The Mechlin ground is squarer and thicker than the Brussels ground which it closely resembles. Width 3ins.

Alençon, 1740. Lappet, showing the laced ground and the thick buttonholing.

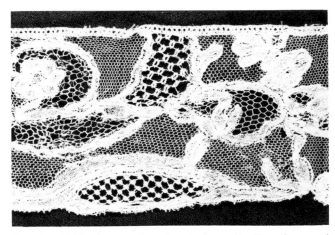

Brussels, 1760. A poor piece, but it shows the Brussels ground clearly, and how it is attached to the motifs. Width 3ins.

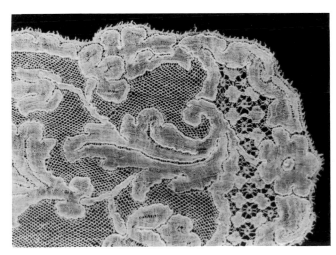

Mechlin, 1740. Lappet with a Mechlin ground: at the end is a mixed ground of snowballs and quatrefoils. The thick thread which distinguishes Mechlin can be clearly seen. No other lace used it; it is the same front and back.

Valenciennes, 1710. The quatrefoil filling stitch much used at Valenciennes contrasts well with the cinq trous ground.

Milan. By the middle of the 18th century the square ground was discovered to be much more economical in thread than any other ground. Most lace makers, from Milan to Valenciennes, hurried to change to this ground, though others were still used. Widths 7½ ins.

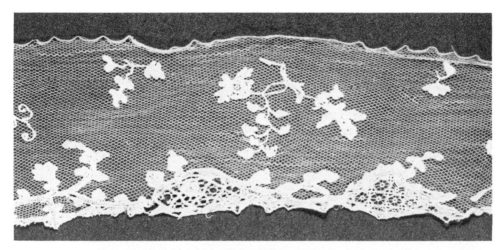

Brussels, 18th century. Alençon needle lace applied to a handmade Brussels ground. Width 3ins.

Brussels, 1820. Needle lace applied to machine net.

Honiton, 1840. Fichu of bobbin lace motifs applied to machine net.

Back view showing the application.

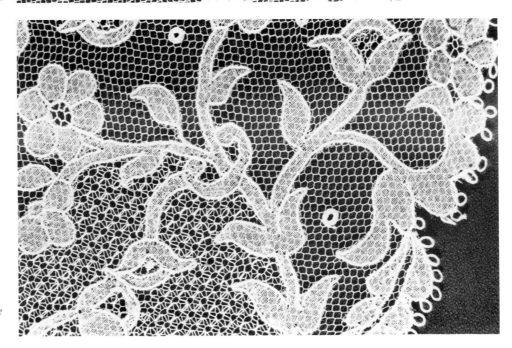

Ireland, Carrickmacross, 1840. Muslin applied with buttonhole stitch.

THREADS

Lace could be, and was, made of many different threads: silk, all through the centuries, wool, cotton, even human hair. Gold and silver threads were much admired for court wear, particularly in the sixteenth and seventeenth centuries. However, most lace was made of flaxen thread. Flax is an annual plant which grows in Northern Europe and as far south as Italy. It can still be seen growing, in small fields, all over Europe. The coats of British soldiers varied in colour during the seventeenth and eighteenth centuries depending on the weather and therefore how well the plants used for dyeing grew: likewise the growth and harvest of flax must have been anxiously watched because of their effect on the quality of the thread.

The thread produced in Flanders, notably at Haarlem, was the finest ever known. This thread was made from the beginning of the fifteenth to the end of the eighteenth century. No-one knows what made it so exceptional. One theory is that the flax itself was slightly different. As it is grown from seed, this could be the case. The other possibility is the exceptional set of conditions under which the thread was made, conditions so intolerable that the workers finally rebelled. There are horrifying stories of thread being spun in dark, damp cellars, with a single ray of light directed on to the work. The dampness was to prevent the thread breaking. No machine has ever been made to spin thread as fine as the handmade threads of the early eighteenth century. This thread was immensely costly; in the middle of that century thread from Haarlem fetched more than £10,000 per pound weight in modern terms. This meant that the raw material of however small a piece of lace was of such value that only the best makers would have been allowed to use it, the highest quality of lace combining the finest thread with the best workmanship. The making of lace was so slow that the client would have expected to wait two or three years for an order to be completed. By the middle of the seventeenth century lace shops were opened and finished lace could be bought. This must have increased trade enormously and made the lace masters even richer.

Italian lace was less fine. Of course thread of different types was sold all over Europe, and no lace can be identified by the thread of which it was made. But the Flemish were unlikely to have imported the best Italian thread; only the cheaper sorts for the mass market being worth their while. On the other hand, the Italians imported the best Flemish thread they could buy for their finest laces.

Towards the end of the eighteenth century machine-made thread and machine-made net were made commercially. It must be remembered that to the eighteenth century mind machine-made net was new, exciting and rare. Designs were adapted to the limitations of the machines and as the machines improved, so the range of design increased. Finally one finds handmade lace copying machine-made lace.

Hand work was, for many years, added to machine-made lace to make the design better. Thick threads were run in to outline leaves and other bits of design. Finally the machine workers learnt how to weave in thick threads. The way to tell the wholly machine-made lace from the handmade additions is to look closely at the thick thread. The hand worker used a long thread to outline a leaf quickly. The machine could work in only one direction and so the outline had to be made with two threads which had to be cut at the tip of the leaf.

Different threads and techniques all have different feels. Woollen lace obviously feels like knitting. Silk lace is crisper than flax or cotton and has the lovely colour of pure, undyed silk. Cotton lace made before 1832 is always frayed looking, as the cotton fibres come up from the thread. After 1832 when it was discovered how to 'cook' the thread to make it stay whole, cotton lace was made which feels softer and less crisp than flaxen lace.

Handmade lace thread is softer to the touch than the thread that was made by machine from late in the 1770s. Richard Arkwright set up his first spinning machine, using water power, in 1771. Machine-made net or lace always has a dry crisp feeling which is quite different from handmade net or lace. When the lace is made on machine-made net, this crisp feeling always remains. It is not starch, or anything added to the net, and it cannot be washed soft.

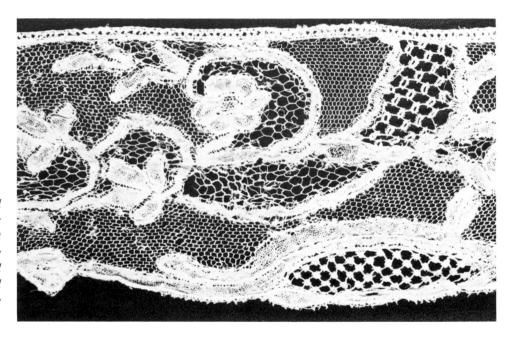

This piece of lace is in such bad condition that it should never appear in any collection, but it shows some original filling and the coarse stitches put in by hurried repairers. Hand working, paid presumably by the piece, must have been exhausting, frustrating work.

COLLECTING

Lace collectors, like all other collectors, should begin by buying as large a quantity as they can afford. In a few months, most of this lace will be understood to be unworthy of collection, but in the interval, the collector will have felt, looked at, and appreciated the good and bad points of the purchase. At the same time, the collector should look at all the lace available in museums and collections. The museums have and show the best that exists; the ordinary collector is unlikely ever to own examples of the finest pieces of the rarest laces. This book shows you the whole range of lace. There are examples of well designed as well as badly designed lace; there are examples of the lace worn every day by ordinary people as well as museum examples of the very best that money could buy. Because the best is rare and costly, collectors should buy any scrap, torn or dirty or too small, in order to handle and look at the best. One day a full repeat in perfect order might turn up somewhere, and if one has studied the scrap, one will recognise the piece. The greatest joy in collecting is in the optimistic feeling that a 'star' will turn up one day.

KEEPING A COLLECTION

The perfect way to house a collection is to put each piece between sheets of acid free tissue paper, or if it is a long flounce or edging to wrap it around a cardboard roll wrapped in the same paper. This is the way the lace is stored at the Victoria and Albert Museum. However, few private houses have dust free cupboards.

I keep my lace in rolls of cotton poplin. I buy three metres and divide it into four pieces of cloth, thirty inches by the width of the poplin. I hem the two raw edges in opposite directions, then I turn the left hand edge in six inches to form a pocket six inches wide which can then be divided to suit the size of the lace being stored. I turn over one and a half inches at the top to make a pocket to be stuffed with plastic foam to make a stiff core. At the bottom, I stitch on two pieces of tape to tie the roll. This roll can hold a large number of pieces of lace with acid free tissue paper. The lace does get crumpled, but a cool iron soon puts that right. The rolls are small enough to fit into a drawer easily and yet big enough to keep a lot of lace clean and tidy.

WASHING LACE

Never wash lace unless you must. If it is very delicate, lay it between layers of nylon net and wash it all together. Most lace can stand ordinary careful washing. Soak it first to loosen the dirt — and get rid of any tea stains. Our predecessors liked ecru lace and the tea colour covered dirty stains that had not washed out, so one should be careful about dyed lace. Occasionally coffee dipped lace appears; this is a disaster as nothing will remove coffee. The tea will come out quickly and will disappear after a couple of changes of water. Then wash the lace in good soap. It is essential to rinse it many times. Where there is much iron in the water, as in London, one needs to use a final rinse in purified water. Very occasionally one needs to boil lace to get rid of a bad stain, but in general this is unnecessary. After washing spread the lace carefully into shape and lay it on a bath towel. The rough surface will help it to dry in shape. A quick press with a cool iron will make it look tidy. Starch is sometimes present in lace; try to wash it out.

CHAPTER II

Italy

The first mention of lace is in a will of 1493. We do not know when lace was first made, nor where, but a great deal of it must have been made in the sixteenth century as so many pattern books were issued then. Many of these could have been used for embroidery, but the majority were clearly meant for the making of bobbin lace.

Several of the earliest, biggest and most famous towns in Italy were built round fine harbours. The countryside behind these towns is usually steep and rocky or volcanic or both and could not supply enough food to feed the people of the port. It therefore became necessary to build up industries to make the money to buy food. Naples was famous for its ribbons; Genoa for its braids. Braids can be very complicated and the techniques for making elaborate braids are very close to the techniques for knotting or macramé and for bobbin lace. We need not be surprised, then, to find bobbin lace developing in Genoa. Genoa was the port that the Spaniards used to supply their troops in the Low Countries. Any novelty must have quickly spread north and south along this route.

The designs of early laces are much the same all over Europe; only the techniques can show where a lace was made. Genoese lace was, to begin with, a straight lace as was the lace of Western Flanders. Part lace was made in Eastern Flanders and, although the laces look the same, it is easy to distinguish them. The straight lace of Western Flanders was later made in Mechlin and Valenciennes, the Eastern lace in Brussels. The United

Ragusa, 1600. Collar. This identification is not entirely convincing; Ragusa lace was very well known but this design seems too naïve for a sophisticated colony of Venice. Length 13ins., width 2¼ins.
The Metropolitan Museum of Art, gift by subscription, 1909. (09.68.102)

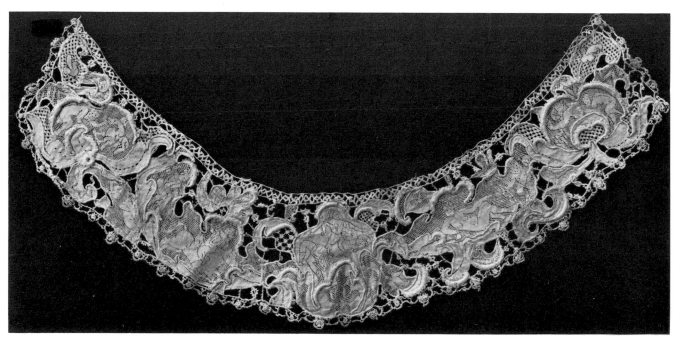

Ragusa, 16th century. Needle lace medallion. The central figure, Christ the Good Shepherd, is surrounded by interlacing and floral ornaments. 6ins. square.
The Metropolitan Museum of Art, gift of Mrs. Magdalena Nuttall, 1908. (08.180.691b)

Provinces also produced a straight lace, made of a very white thread. The design books printed in Venice showed designs for bobbin lace, which must have been made by amateurs. After 1580 there were no design books, so we must assume that lace making had become a profession and that lace manufacturers had built up the trade so that no amateur could compete.

The Venetian lace that we recognise is all needle lace: we do not know whether any bobbin lace was made there. If it was, it may be that it is indistinguishable from Milanese lace to our eyes. Another mystery is the style of the lace from Ragusa which, although it was a Venetian town, is mentioned as having lace distinct from that of Venice. Again we do not know what it looked like. Sicily was far famed for its embroidery but we do not know if any lace was made there; yet professional embroiderers would have had no difficulty in making needle lace. We are also told of lace made at Rome, but the fine bobbin lace called point de Rome must be Flemish since it is made in many pieces with many cut ends of threads.

EARLY ITALIAN NEEDLE LACE

As described in Chapter One, needle lace must have developed from embroidery used to decorate a hem. First a hole could be made by pulling the fabric in several directions, then a hole could be cut, its edges neatened with buttonhole stitch, then the hole could be filled with a decoration and that would have been the earliest kind of needle lace. Gradually the workers freed themselves first of the actual cloth and then of the idea of rigid right-angles. Then, and only then, could the pattern have been drawn onto vellum with curves; the outlines stitched on and the spaces filled with a variety of stitches. These stages are clearly shown in the following illustrations: pulled fabric holes, cut work, i.e. square holes edged with buttonhole stitch and filled with needle lace, narrow borders joined with needle lace, more and more elaborate cut work, but still contained by the fabric; then finally it was discovered how to make curves.

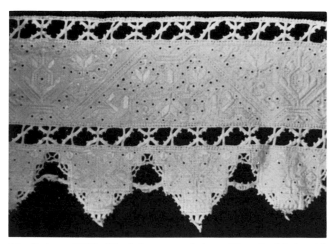

Needle lace, 1575. The holes are made by pulling the fabric with stitches. The inserts are needle lace, holding the linen together. Width 5ins.

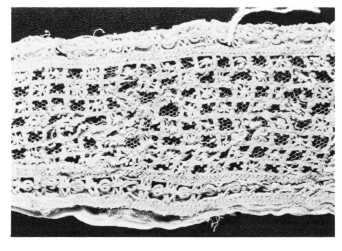

This frail piece mounted on net was originally part of a piece of linen. The pulled thread and cut work are held by the fabric threads. Width 2½ ins.

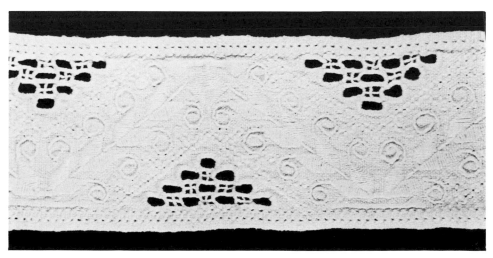

The cut work holes are balanced by elaborate surface stitchery. Width 2ins.

The design is still part of the fabric. Width 1½ins.

A corner of a tablecloth. Linen stitching edges the piece and the cutwork is elaborate.

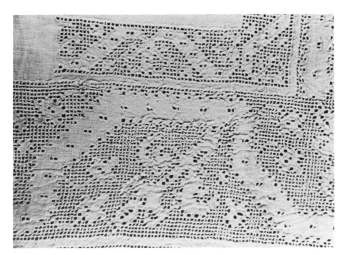

Drawn thread work.

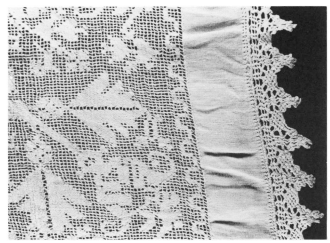

Drawn thread work with a needle lace border.

Needle lace border on a drawn thread work cloth.

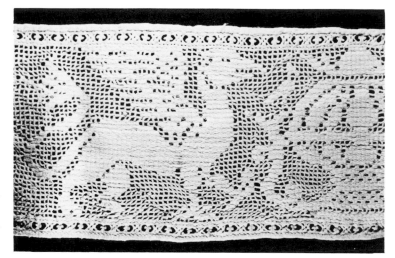

1600. Pulled thread work; the threads that are left are covered with buttonhole stitch and the design is darned in. Width 5ins.

Buratto. The loose woven ground was darned to make the design. Width 13½ins.

Drawn thread work with darned design. Width 11½ins.

Plate 11. Lacis, 1650. Brilliantly coloured appliqué on red net. Width 6½ins.

Early Italian lace was made both with the needle and with bobbins. Like the lace all over Europe at the same time, it was either narrow insertion or sharply scalloped. The light laces were used on dress and the heavier ones on furnishing, either religious or secular. The early needle lace worked on linen is very beautiful and elaborate. The reticella of the same date is as fine as its Flemish counterpart. They are incomparable laces. There were other Italian laces of the sixteenth and seventeenth centuries that were no longer made when mesh laces came into fashion. The most beautiful is punto in aria (in air, or made of air). The design is always superb and so is the workmanship. There is very little of it. It must have taken forever to work and have cost the earth when finished! Another lace is 'lacis' which is made either onto a knotted or woven mesh. Appliqué and darning stitches were added. Lacis was usually made in colours and does not look much like the fabric we think of as lace. In addition, there was a white lace, also darned onto a woven mesh. It has charming designs, showing people and houses and animals and birds. It seems to have been much used for bed-hangings, since the pieces are often enormous.

Right and below: Very similar bobbin lace borders on needle lace. Width 6ins.

Width 3ins.

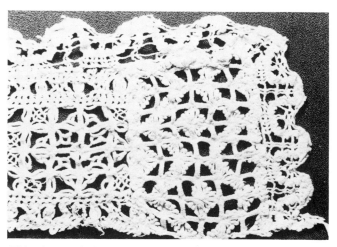

This zig-zag design first appeared about 1550. Width 2½ins.

EARLY ITALIAN BOBBIN LACE

The many lace pattern books of the sixteenth century make it easy to date early bobbin lace. Bobbin lace was first made early in the seventeenth century in large quantities all over Northern Italy. We divide it into that made under the influence of Milan and that made under the influence of Genoa. Both sorts of lace were made over wide areas and the making of it does not appear to have been controlled in the way that it was in Brussels.

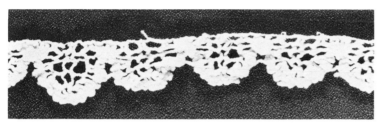

Bobbin lace. Width ½ in.

The 'cherry' design is to be found in many books. Width 1½ ins.

Needle lace. Border 2¼ ins., corner 4¼ ins.

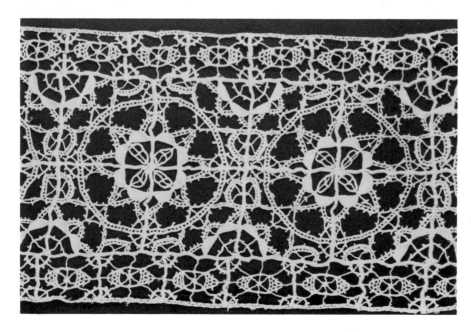

Reticella. The design is very close to one in the Vecellio Pattern Book, Venice 1592. Width 4ins.

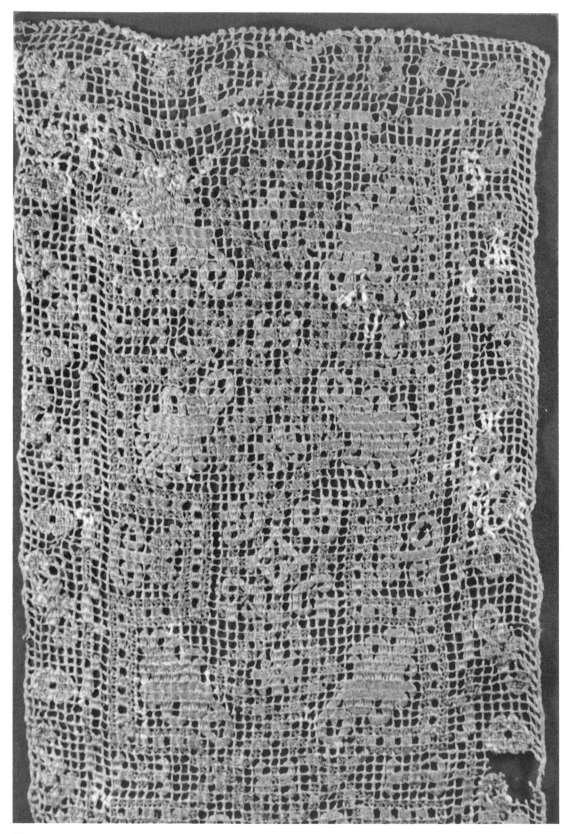

Plate 12. Lacis, 1650. Possibly made further north, in Germany. These curious coloured laces came from many places and there is no sure way of identifying where they were made.

Bobbin lace, late 16th century. Border with geometrical wheel of forms. Length 112ins., width 4ins.

The Metropolitan Museum of Art, gift of Mrs. R.W. de Forest, 1935. (35.108.10)

Above: 1610. The design is still based on the right angled threads of woven linen. Width 7ins.

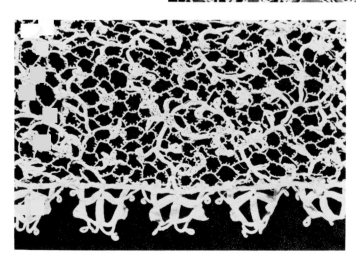

A bobbin border on a large piece of needle lace. Width 12ins.

A needle lace border on a bobbin lace piece. Width 6ins.

Needle lace, late 16th century. Border with different motifs repeated. Length 2yds. 7ins., width 3ins.
The Metropolitan Museum of Art, gift by subscription, 1909. (09.68.92)

Bobbin lace, late 16th century. Plaited linen edging, with alternating figures of man and woman in band with deep hanging points on lower edge. Length 14ins., width 2ins., with 3½ins. deep points.
The Metropolitan Museum of Art, gift of Lady Reigate in memory of her mother, Mrs. William Redmond Cross, 1979. (1979.310.15)

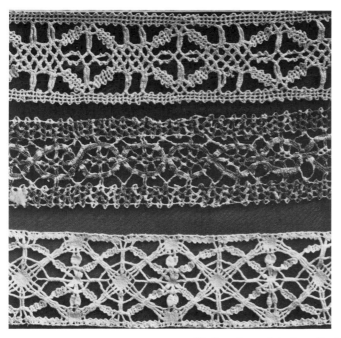

All these laces date from the 1580s to '90s.
The Metropolitan Museum of Art, gift of Mrs. Nuttall, 1908. (08.180.500)

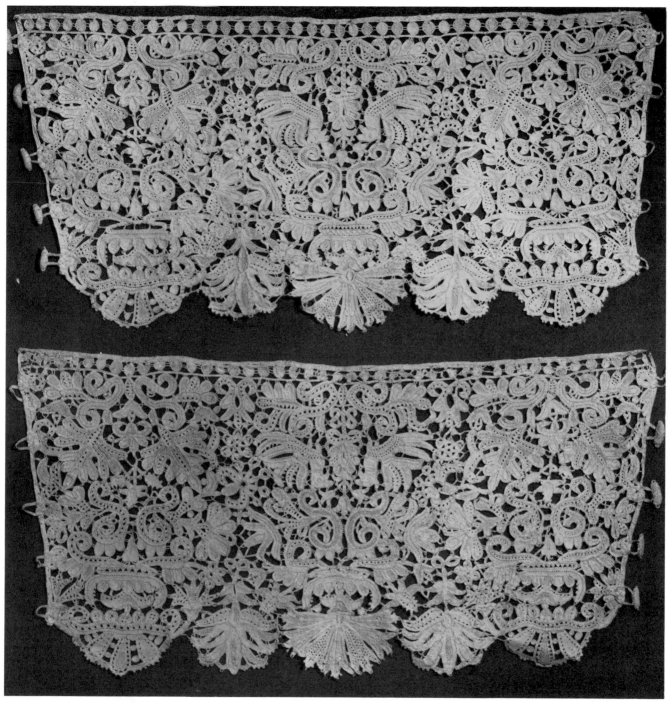

Bobbin and needle lace, 17th century. Cuffs. Punto in aria — the elegant curves are very beautiful.
The Metropolitan Museum of Art, gift of Mrs. Edward S. Harkness, 1930. (30.135.155)

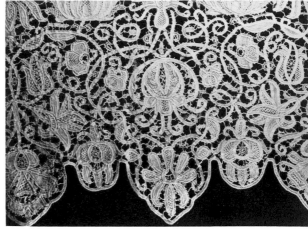

Bobbin lace. 16th century. Linen edging. A most interesting enlargement showing how the threads flow through the work.
The Metropolitan Museum of Art, gift of Mrs. Edward S. Harkness, 1930. (30.135.137)

Punto in aria, a needle lace of great beauty. It is rarely seen, but is always of superlative design and workmanship. The designs are not handicapped by being based on right angles. Width 8ins.

Five 17th century pieces, including centre, punto in aria, oval frame enclosing a branch with two birds with black bead eyes. Height 5¾ins., width 4ins.
The Metropolitan Museum of Art, gift of Mrs. Nuttall, 1908. (08.180.500)

Needle lace, 17th century. Ten pieces, all punto in aria.
The Metropolitan Museum of Art, anonymous gift, 1879. (79.1.208,210,222)

GENOA

Genoa was one of the many city states of sixteenth century Italy. The barrenness of the countryside around the town had earlier caused the development of sea trade and banking to pay for the food of its people. It became a rich town and, as in Naples, its people created what we would call luxury goods. Genoa was famous for its gold and silver lace and for braids. The making of these textiles prepared the way for the making of bobbin lace with flaxen thread. Certainly many of the sixteenth century narrow laces were more like braids than lace as we think of it. These narrow insertions soon developed into the wider scalloped laces much used on collars at the beginning of the seventeenth century. In the middle of the century appeared the wide and very beautiful laces which were so much appreciated.

During the seventeenth century, Genoa was controlled by Spain. Genoa declared itself a free port in 1608, but Spain still needed Genoa as a port, along with Leghorn, to supply her armies stationed all across Europe to the Spanish Netherlands. Thus there was much travelling between the Spanish possessions in the Low Countries and the Mediterranean. It does not seem unreasonable to guess that lace makers, too, travelled between the Spanish Netherlands and Genoa. Genoese lace is made all in one piece (straight lace), as was the lace of Valenciennes and Binche. This is a complicated and difficult technique and it was not used in any other Italian town. The

An early piece of Genoese lace. It is a straight lace and the threads are carried in the wide solid piece between the scallops. Width 2¼ins.

Below: The scallops become gradually more and more elaborate. Width 3ins.

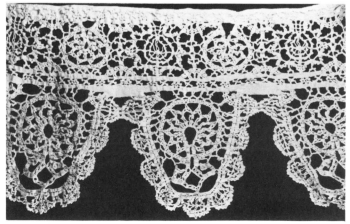

A typical piece of fine 'collar lace' of about 1620. Width 6½ins.

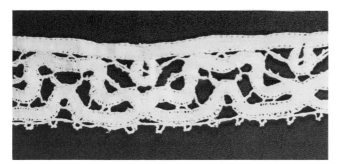

A straight lace with typical bars. Width 1½ins.

This very fine border on a collar shows the elaborate geometric designs possible. Width 4½ins.

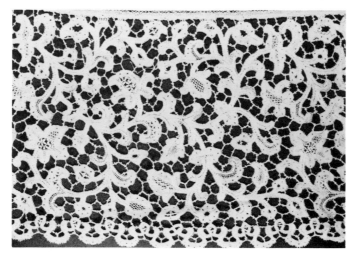

1700. A lovely lace with many fillings. Note the characteristic border. Width 6ins.

designs are lovely. The shapes are big, but the whole is speckled with holes between the pieces of the design, and many different stitches are used within the pieces. Again, one can see links with the early designs of Valenciennes and Binche. The overall effect is quite different from lace made at Milan. It looks light-hearted and less formal.

There were three main types. First the lace was designed without bars with many lovely fillings. This was a sophisticated stylish lace. Then swirling flower or bird shapes were linked by double bars. These distinctive double bars were made by joining the piece of design to the end of one bar with a tiny hook which slipped a loop through a prepared hole; the loop could be knotted and the second half of the double bar made back to the original bit of design. The third type was a busy lace. The tape was made with the rest of the lace and curls back on itself. This is carefully described by Margaret Jourdain in her book *Old Lace*.

The later laces have a lovely shaped border, which makes the lace look lighter than it really is. Presumably this was done in an effort to follow the fashion of light lace created in France. The sumptuary laws and customs duties were heavily laid against foreign lace so that Genoese lace was worn at home, and there is little mention of its export in the eighteenth century.

Genoese lace is distinctive both in design and technique. Many pieces have small wheatears tucked into sometimes incongruous places and these add to the speckled appearance. When it was decided to teach lace making in Malta in the early nineteenth century, teachers were sent from Genoa and these wheatears became a mark of Maltese lace. Maltese lace was made of coarser thread than that used at Genoa and, with the addition of the cross of Saint John, the resulting lace can easily be distinguished from the Genoese.

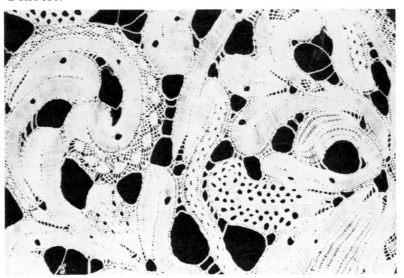

Straight lace with many filling stitches and very simple bars. Width 9ins.

Bobbin lace, late 17th-early 18th century. An insertion of Genoese tape lace. Length 127½ins., width 8ins.
The Metropolitan Museum of Art, anonymous gift, 1949. (49.32.19)

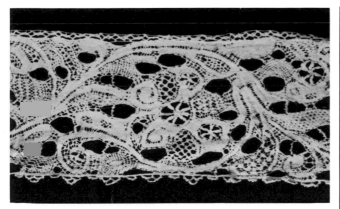

1630. Only a few elaborate bars and many elaborate filling stitches in this piece. Width 3ins.

Bobbin lace, 1640. Made with many fillings. Width 8½ins.

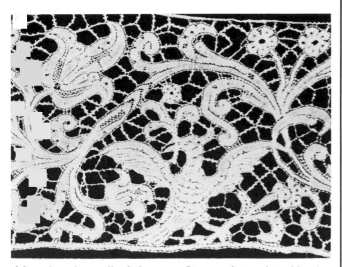

Many bars here, all of the same Genoese shape, date this piece 1660. Width 5½ins.

Again, many fillings; the ground is of bars and wheatears. Width 7ins.

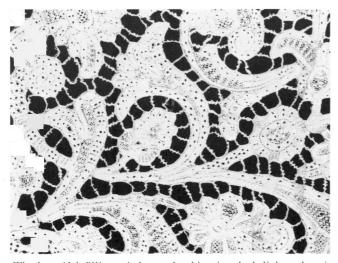

The beautiful filling stitches make this piece look lighter than it really is. Width 9ins.

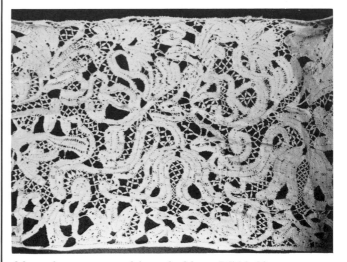

More wheatears are used instead of bars. Width 9ins.

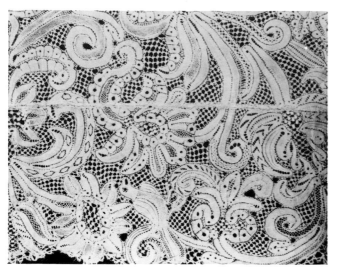

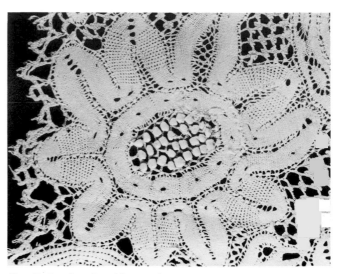

1750. This handsome piece was cut in half and then put together again. Width 9½ ins.

Detail showing the odd ground.

Bobbin lace, 18th century. Border with design of sirens, birds and scrolls; the toile is ornamented with knots. Length 3yds. 20ins., width 6ins.
The Metropolitan Museum of Art, Rogers Fund, 1908. (08.48.15)

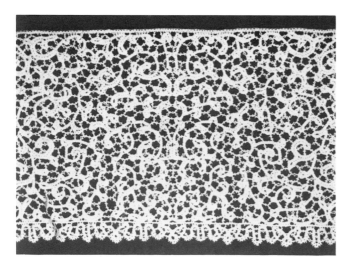

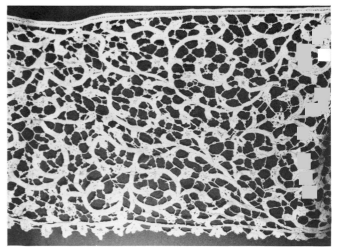

1720. A mirrored design made with many twists and turns. Width 6¾ ins.

1760. The bars are even more elaborate. The designs are becoming confused. Width 8½ ins.

Four strips, early 18th century. The third border down has scrolling branch with stag, dog, bird and pomegranates (the centres in knot stitch). Length 26ins., width 3ins.
The Metropolitan Museum of Art, Rogers Fund, 1920. (20.186.342)

MILAN

Milan was a large town in the seventeenth century; it was also the centre of a large dukedom. The Dukes of Milan, the Sforzas, knew how to conquer territory and how to hold it. In 1493 lace trimmed linen was divided between Angela and Ippolita Sforza Visconti in a deed of 'partitioni' which is the earliest known mention of lace. There seems no doubt that what we call lace was meant. Once lace had become an exportable commodity, lace making must have been organised in a businesslike way. It was made by more than 100,000 people in the Dukedom, country and town, and an immense quantity of Milanese lace, good, bad and indifferent was made.

The best Milanese lace is very beautiful. It was not designed as a pretty lace. The designs are often of Renaissance derivation, and come from famous design books such as Guarino Guarini's book on architecture, and other Flemish and Italian books. The designers were not attempting pretty frothy lace, but a solid beautiful textile which could be spread onto a table or worn at the bottom of an alb. The designs began without bars, then bars appeared and gradually turned into mesh. In the eighteenth century a square mesh was used and the designs became more informal. There are enchanting pictures of country life, or court life, and many beautiful very

Above: 1640. Bobbin lace made with a minimum of bars. Width 4ins.

Above right: 1650. Pretty double bars join the pieces. Width 7ins.

1660. Not a mesh, but bars. Width 7½ins.

natural flowers, though even then the scrolling shapes were all important. The lace was made from a pale cream coloured thread with a very smooth feel to it.

Milanese lace was made in vast quantities and the standards were not guarded. The lace was made all at the same time; it is not a straight lace, as threads were added and subtracted to swell the graceful loops, but the ground was not made separately as there are no plaits or loops of threads on the back. Most of the Milanese lace in the sale rooms is poor in design, but usually well made. It is evidently a long lasting lace. There is an enormous amount of it on the market.

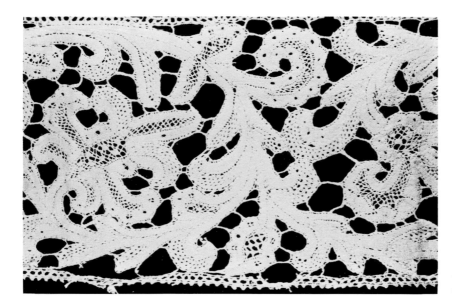

1640. Another early piece with bars. Width 4½ ins.

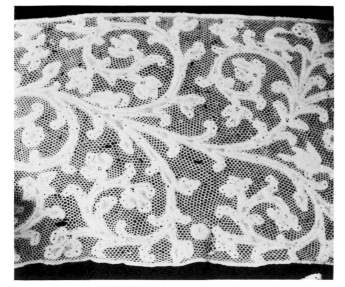

A wandering ground. Width 14½ ins.

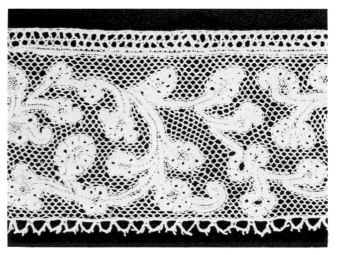

The ground here is almost neat and tidy. Width 3ins.

The double curving tapes have added threads to increase the curve. Width 10ins.

There are many beautiful filling stitches here. Width 6½ins.

A typical design of the best period, circa 1710. This is a superb piece of lace. Width 7½ins.

Early 18th century. The lovely natural flowers in these laces are well displayed though the ground still wanders slightly. Width 7½ins.

Width 7½ins.

Width 7½ins.

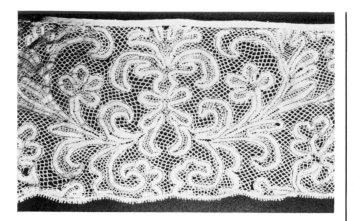

These run of the mill pieces show the good, bad and indifferent designs. Such large quantities of lace were made in and around Milan that one would expect this range. Widths all 5½ins.

The vague design makes this a poor piece of lace. Width 13ins.

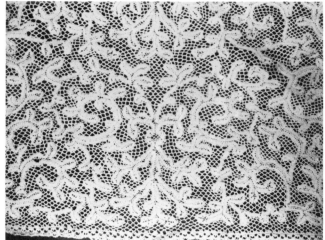

1750. There are traces of a mirrored design. An early tape lace with a ground that has not yet settled. Width 10ins. showing.

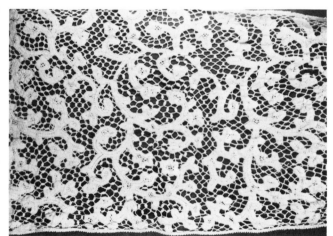

An unusual ground with wheatears at some crossings in the mesh. Width 8½ins.

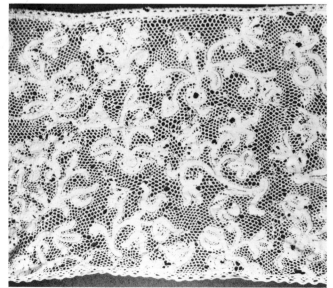

1675. A charming design with a large number of stitches. The fashionable clothes with all the detail are very like those in the stumpwork embroidery of England at the same period.
Victoria and Albert Museum.

1750. This square showing a scene from ordinary life may have been used to decorate a bed hanging. 15½ ins. square.

VENICE

During the sixteenth century, it was the custom all over Europe for the grandeur of a noble to be measured by the size of his household. This was sustained longer in Venice than elsewhere. The women of the households did the sewing and embroidery, as did those women, including nuns, who lived in convents. The lace making took place in households and convents and was organised by lace dealers. It was immensely important to the financial situation in the city.

At first Venetian lace swept the world. Venetian needle lace is regarded as being the most beautiful ever made. The designs are elaborate, with elegant curves, and can only be compared with the designs on Persian carpets and tiles. There is no attempt at all to imitate nature in the curved, interlocking shapes. The technique is wonderful. The very finest threads were used to build up shapes that, like the English stumpwork of the time, are almost three dimensional. The English work was, of course, based on natural, every day objects, whereas the Venetian work is almost abstract in design.

In the early seventeenth century one of the best of all laces, gros point de Venise, came into being. It seems three dimensional, made of thread so fine that the motifs look as if they had been carved in ivory. During the nineteenth century this lace was so highly regarded that it was often 'altered', that is, the motifs were cut apart and rearranged, often with other bits added to make the piece bigger. Gros point was made until the middle of the eighteenth century with little change in design.

There were several other types of Venetian lace. Rosepoint has smaller flowers and small cordonnets and more elaborate bars. Point de neige has smaller flowers still, with even more elaborate bars. Obviously one bought the size of lace that was needed; for instance, heavy gros point to be seen from a distance on an altar frontal, the finer ones for dress.

Needle lace, late 17th century. Flounce in gros point.
The Metropolitan Museum of Art, gift of Mrs. William H. Bliss, 1914. (14.69)

There were also two types of flat lace. Point plat is a beautiful scrolled lace with wonderfully elaborate fillings and no padding. Coralline is smaller and less exciting, a confused lace with no style or charm, a poor substitute for point plat.

For the first hundred years Venice had no rival. When, in 1665, the French minister, Colbert, ordered the setting up of lace making schools, the Venetians were annoyed but made no effort to retaliate. By 1690, however, they found that their ladies preferred French lace, and that they had lost export markets.

The popularity of Venetian lace in the seventeenth century caused many countries to pass laws intended to protect them from spending vast sums of money in Venice. Like all such laws, they were not obeyed. Venice continued to grow rich on lace. The designs changed little in the seventeenth and early eighteenth centuries. The French, under Colbert, learnt the techniques of Venice and produced better designed and lighter lace. By 1700 they had changed the whole nature of lace from a heavy material intended to lie flat into something light and gathered. In spite of frantic efforts by the Venetians to ban the import of foreign lace, French lace continued to be bought in, and their own lace was no longer selling on the export market. It was economic disaster for Venice. Desperately they turned to a new lighter lace, point de Venise à reseau, to give it its nineteenth century title. It is an incredibly delicate and beautiful lace. The designs are lovely and it has a light ground made not across but lengthwise which makes it easily distinguishable from all other laces. Some experts think that this lace was made in northern Europe and not in Venice, but the ground is worked as the Burano ground was worked in the later eighteenth century, which would indicate otherwise. This lovely lace was not appreciated and lace making in Venice gradually faded out in the middle of the eighteenth century.

This typical piece of gros point is of the type that 19th century collectors named point d'ivoire. Width 3¾ins. The 19th century passion for names and, in English, French names, is a confusing factor in lace collecting. The first lace collectors were French and when lace collecting was taken up in England and America it became the snobbish thing to interlard the collecting language with French. Wherever possible English should now be used.

Venetian lace was made in all sizes. The earliest was designed without bars. Bars were generally introduced and became more and more elaborate as the century went on. This piece has a few bars and is therefore later than the piece to the left. It is less fine; there are fewer different filling stitches and the design is less well organised. Width 4ins.

Venetian lace was so highly valued in the nineteenth century that it received much attention from the 'repairers' of the time. It is not easy to find a piece of Venetian lace which has not been altered. Obviously the very heavy laces held together by light bars did need constant repair while they were in use. Now age has damaged the threads so some repairs are necessary, but there was no justification for the remaking that went on a hundred years ago. Venetian lace should have a repeat like any other lace, but this is nowadays not easily found.

Carved by Grinling Gibbons (1648-1721) this bow, made in imitation of Venetian lace of the mid-17th century, was once worn at court by Horace Walpole (1717-1797). Gibbons made nine or ten of these from limewood.

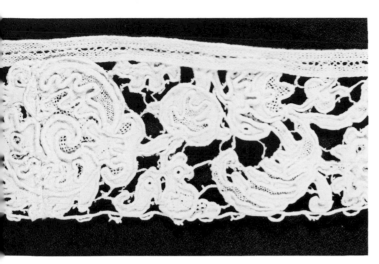

A poor battered piece, but interesting as it has so few bars. Width 1¾ins.

More bars, and more elaborate ones. Width 2¾ins.

A great many bars, and several elaborate ones. Width 4ins.

A much finer piece than the one above, it has a long repeat. Width 4ins.

The corner of a collar. The beautifully balanced design, apparently mounted on its original linen, is sufficiently sophisticated not to have a mirrored corner.

Still an S shaped design, but with very elaborate stitchery. Width 3ins.

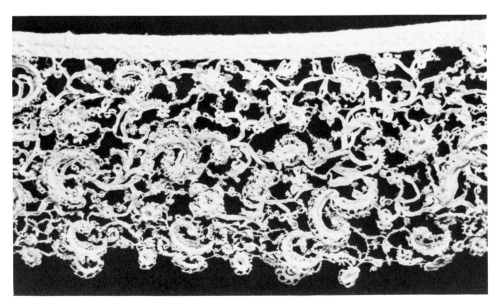

This very fine lace depends on superb technique for effect. This was called rosepoint or even point de neige. Both are fancy names that mean little. Width 3ins.

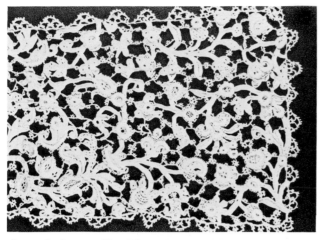

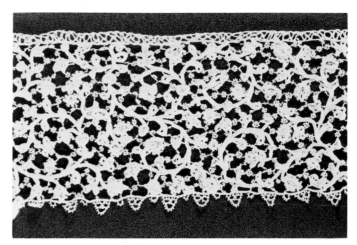

One end of a mantilla. The exuberance of Venetian needle lace is enchanting. Width 4½ins.

Here the basic S shapes can be clearly seen. Width 3ins.

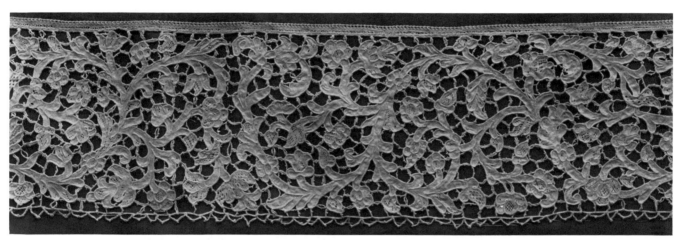

Needle lace, 17th to 18th century. Border of flat lace, bobbin lace edging.
The Metropolitan Museum of Art, anonymous gift, 1949. (49.32.17)

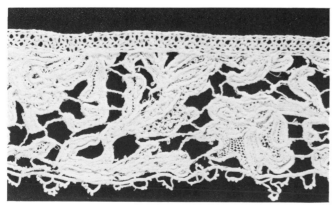

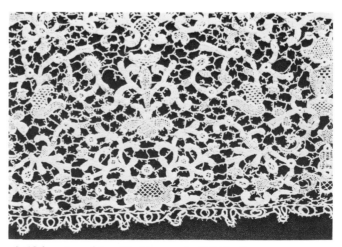

A worn piece of lace but fascinating. It is a 17th century fake piece of bobbin lace with cords added to look like real Venetian needle lace. Width 1¾ins.

A 19th century fake. Machine made. Width 4ins.

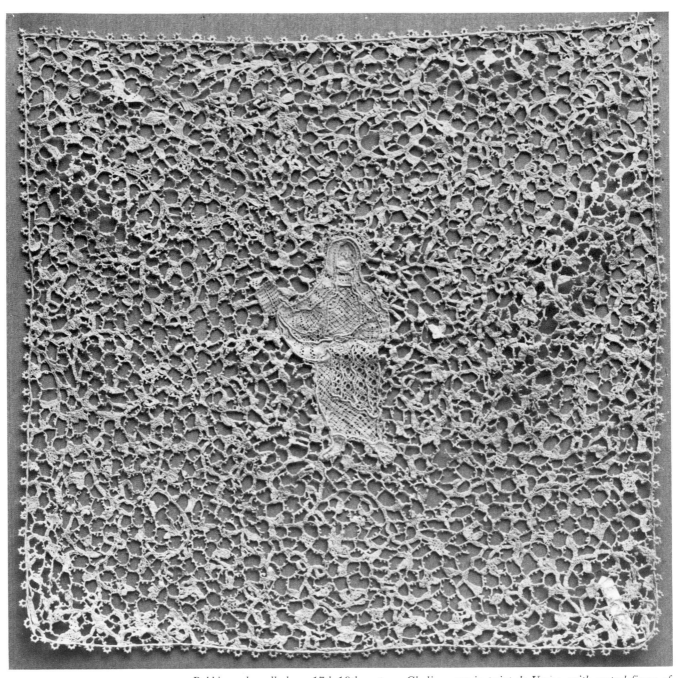

Bobbin and needle lace, 17th-18th century. Chalice cover in point de Venise, with central figure of Saint in bobbin lace with cordonnet outlines. 10ins. square.
The Metropolitan Museum of Art, gift of Mrs. Albert Blum, 1953. (53.162.38)

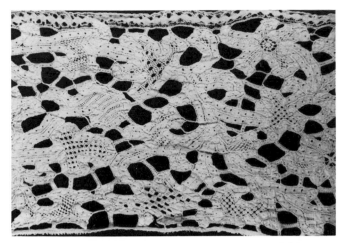

The flat laces of Venice were also beautifully made. This early piece of 1640 has many filling stitches. Width 5ins.

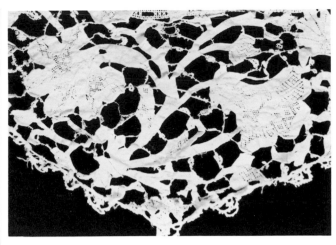

The corner of a collar; this is of very fine quality with some elaborate bars.

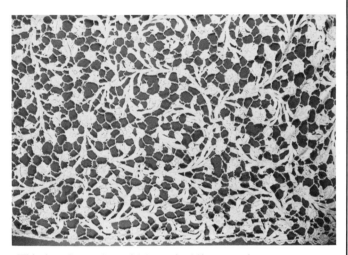

This is a huge piece of lace; only 11ins. are shown.

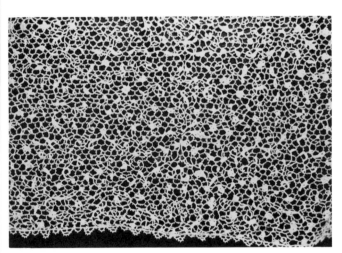

Coralline, 1690. A flat lace of no distinction, but finely worked. The design is very dreary. Width 8¼ins.

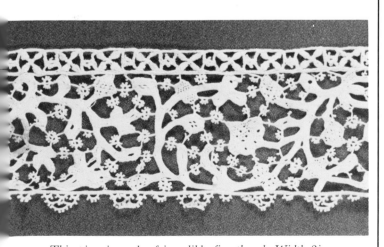

This piece is made of incredibly fine thread. Width 2ins.

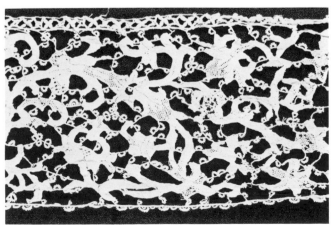

Another piece made of very fine thread. Width 3¼ins.

Mantilla, 1660. As with the raised lace, the bars became more and more elaborate.

A nice piece of flat lace with masses of 19th century bits added to it. Width 3½ins.

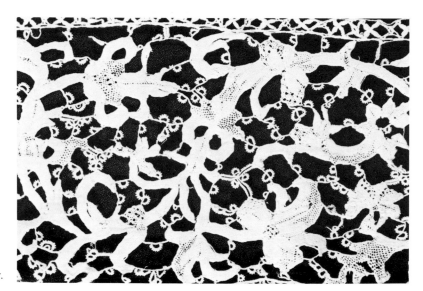

Width 2ins.

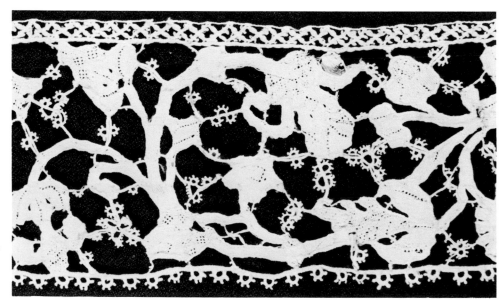

There is a lot of this flat lace and it varies very much in quality. Width 3¼ins.

Needle lace, 18th century. The border second from top is in flat lace with a bobbin heading and scallops on the lower edge, and has graceful scrolls branching from the central ornament. Length 14ins., width 2½ins. The two lower pieces are from Burano.

The Metropolitan Museum of Art, gift of Mrs. Nuttall, 1908. (08.180.707)

Needle lace, 18th century. Two silk squares with ornamental scrolls around central ornament of a cock, and two borders.
The Metropolitan Museum of Art, bequest of Mrs. Jesse Seligman, 1910. (10.102.117-119)

About 1700 the Venetians tried to retrieve their lost lace markets by creating a light lace. This pretty lace was the result, but alas it did not recover their markets. The ground is worked lengthwise as was the ground of Burano lace. Width 3ins.

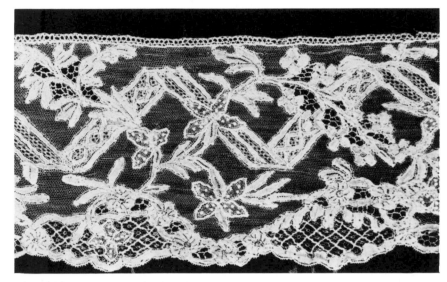

This beautiful lace with its floating ribbons and delicate flowers has an elegant shaped edge. It must have been very pretty gathered in ruffles around the neck of a dress. On the other hand, when put down flat it does not, basically, have a good design. The flowers are not based on drawings from nature and ribbons do not twist in these odd ways. The lace has a lovely feel and touch to it, and is very delicate and fragile looking. Width 3ins.

Two pieces of point de Venise à reseau. There is little buttonhole edging on the motifs and in the top one the familiar zig-zag design can be seen in several places.
The Metropolitan Museum of Art, bequest of Mrs. Jesse Seligman, 1910. (10.102.77)

The design is made for a ruffled lace; flat, it is not very interesting. Width 1½ ins.

Width 3¼ ins.

This shows the lengthwise ground, the sawtoothed filling stitch and the picoted bars, all characteristic of this lace. Width 3¼ ins.

CHAPTER III

France

Lace making in France is said to have been practised from earliest times. There are records of many towns where lace was made in the sixteenth century, but no one can point to a piece of lace and identify it as French and made at that time. In the sixteenth and seventeenth centuries, Flanders was the richest area in Europe; a large middle class was developing, money came in with trade and banking, transport was good and money circulated. In France, on the other hand, transport was so bad that famines were frequent. Plenty of food was grown, but its distribution was so poorly arranged that no one could prevent the devastation that occurred from time to time. Thus famines would occur in one part of France while there was too much food in another area. A famine north of Paris is even mentioned in Pepys' Diary. Colbert, Louis XIV's minister, organized the lace trade and the tapestry trade among others, but he never even tried to organize transport and farming. It was clearly too difficult. Lace makers who brought in money must have been very necessary to their families since if a crop failed money to buy food was vital and lace making was the only source of supply. A lace maker's hands needed to be soft and clean and she cannot have been able to do heavy work on the farm. This must have been irritating in good times. Life in rural France was very hard and near starvation level at the best of times, and as taxes were not paid by the clergy or nobles, the French Revolution cannot have come as a complete surprise.

French lace, like French tapestries, or French porcelain, owes everything to Colbert. France, when Louis XIV was a boy, was still divided up into areas separated by customs posts and tolls. These divisions lasted throughout his reign and Colbert, able though he was, never succeeded, indeed never appears to have tried, to break them down. When Colbert took office, France was poverty stricken. The poor lived at subsistence level, and the rich were very rich. A great deal of rich people's money went to other countries for luxuries unobtainable in France. Sumptuary laws were brought in; as always they were not obeyed. Colbert then started various

Below: The tiny animals on this narrow border are derived from designs by Bérain, the great French designer. They prepare the way for the finest pieces of lace of the period decorated with the King, Louis XIV, and his crown. Width 1½ ins.

Below left: Mirrored designs came early — 1680. These are not fine pieces of lace; they show what would have been worn every day. Width 2¼ ins.

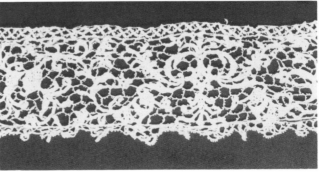

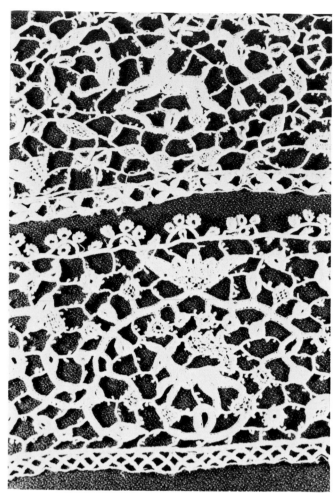

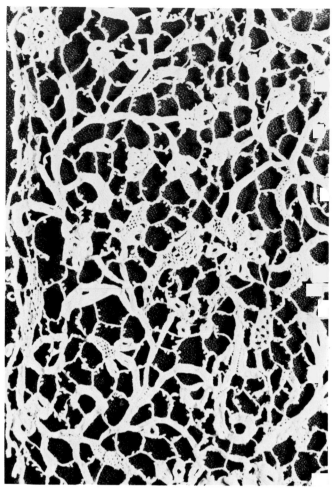

The quality of these small animals made on ordinary lace indicate to what heights the finest lace reached. Width 1½ ins.

Lappet. The ¾ in. bird in the middle of this piece is so out of place that one wonders if it was on the original design. Width 3 ins.

luxury businesses. His method was to allow a monopoly, without taxes, for ten years to certain named people. This he did for various crafts including lace. To help the lace manufacturers, he imported various workers to teach. We know that workers were brought from Venice because the Council there were so outraged by Colbert's success that they passed all sorts of laws to get their workers home and to prevent any others leaving. We know that workers were imported from Flanders, but it is impossible to tell if these workers taught the weaving of woollen cloth or the making of bobbin lace. Before 1665, lace was made in fourteen towns in France. These were helped by Colbert who supplied Venetian or Flemish teachers, who were required at first to use designs prepared in Paris.

Early French lace and Venetian lace should look identical, since the Venetians were teaching the French. As so often in lace, the technique makes the two laces quite distinctive. The picots on French lace are differently made from the Venetian picots. The French picots are smooth ended, while the Venetian ones have a knob or bit of knot on the point. The French designs soon left the Venetian ones behind. They are light-hearted with tiny animals and dancing figures suddenly appearing in the most unlikely places; pieces of lace with apparently little pattern to them will blossom with a deer or duck, which is not repeated and seems to have been put in 'freehand'. The pomposity of Venice did not last.

New ideas were quickly adapted by each place to its own techniques and the result was that each town developed a distinctive style. French lace became the best in Europe: a great triumph for France. Venetian lace disappeared, in spite of the Council requiring it to be worn in public. French people bought what they could afford, and the economy flourished. The revocation of the edict of Nantes in 1685 caused much suffering among lace makers in the North. Many of them were Protestants, but most of them were too poor to escape. The good silversmiths or porcelain makers could escape to England, where they did much to enrich their trades, but the poor lace makers had to stay and get what work they could. A few lace makers may have come to England, but there is no record of them. English lace was made by English workers.

At the end of the seventeenth century, the high fontange, a head-dress with stiffened loops of lace standing up on the head above the cap, went out of fashion and soft muslin became the rage. Lace workers suffered and when the fashion for lace did return some ten years later, it looked almost solid like muslin. However, the beauty of the designs made lace popular again. Grounds were introduced and lace became even lighter and more beautiful. Designs followed fashion: chinoiserie in the 1730s and '40s; rococo followed, but classical ideas and the revolution brought the death knell to lace.

Napoleon loved lace and tried to bring it back into fashion, but by that time the techniques were almost forgotten; the lace he ordered for Josephine was used by Marie Louise.

Paris continued throughout the nineteenth century to be the centre of

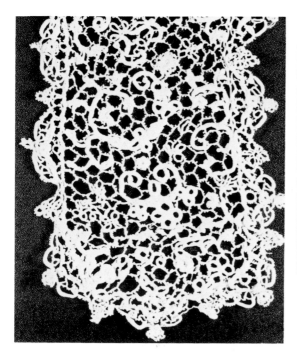

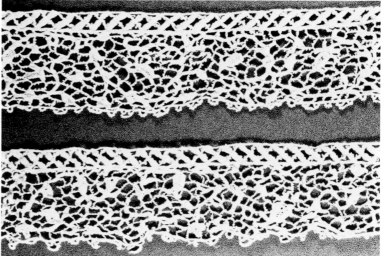

Lappet. These pieces have little design and are very ordinary indeed, but in 1680 lace was precious, however ordinary. Width 3¾ins.

Width 1in.

fashion for Europe. All the big lace manufacturers set up offices in Paris and directed the designs of their workers from there so as to be in the forefront of fashion. Handmade lace continued to be made in bulk until near the end of the century. By using machine-made net as a base for applied lace and embroidery, lace was produced more cheaply and so became available to an ever growing market. By the middle of the century, machine-made lace was also being made in quantity, but to begin with, it needed a lot of hand finishing which kept the quality of design and workmanship comparable to handmade lace. By the 1870s, the competition was such that Chantilly, where a lace easily copied on a machine was made, had to cease production. Much the same sort of thing happened in Valenciennes, though there narrow edgings continued to be made. Thus by 1900, there was little handmade lace being made, only an occasional outstanding piece.

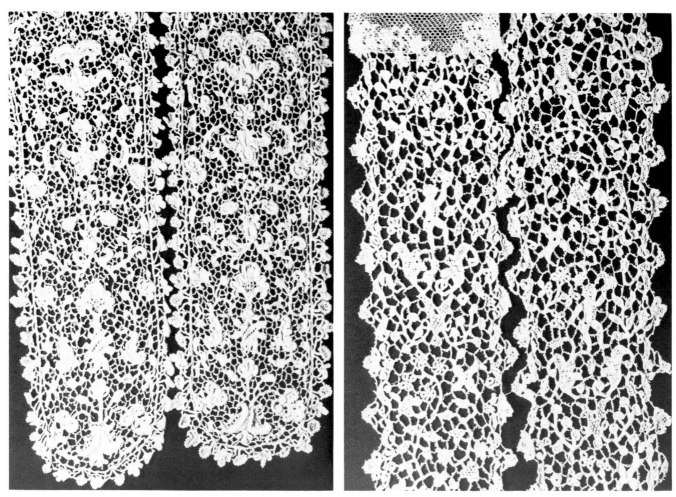

Two pairs of lappets, 1680-90. The left-hand pair has been much altered in the 19th century with dozens of bits added on. The basic design is, however, clear and is so much finer than the Venetian lace of the same period. The right hand pair shows three merry gentlemen. This picture is of the ends of the lappets only: they would have been about five feet long with the centre section looped up into five loops, either on wires or with starch, on the top of the head. The finest pieces of point de France are immensely elegant with well balanced designs showing everything from the king on his horse to a baby in its cot, from fountains to crowns, and all floating in 'trees' or 'seaweed'.

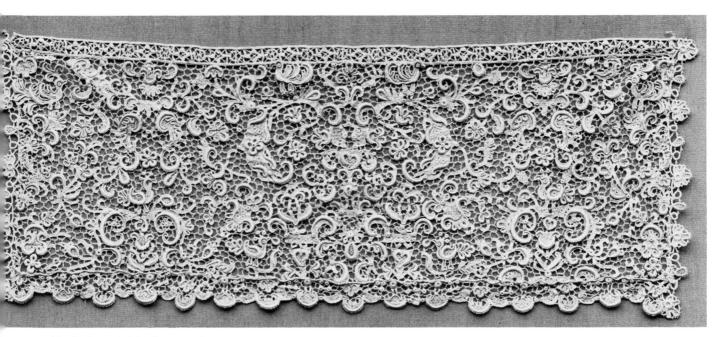

Needle lace, 1670. Cravat end.
The Metropolitan Museum of Art, gift by subscription, 1909. (09.68.158)

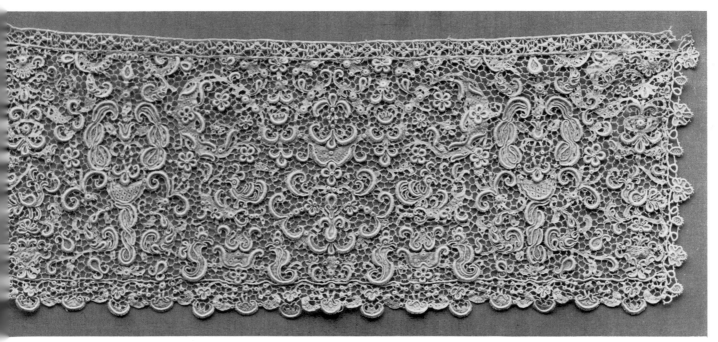

Needle lace, 1670. Cravat end incorporating the monogram of Louis XIV. Length 15½ins., width 6ins.
The Metropolitan Museum of Art, gift by subscription, 1909. (09.68.159)

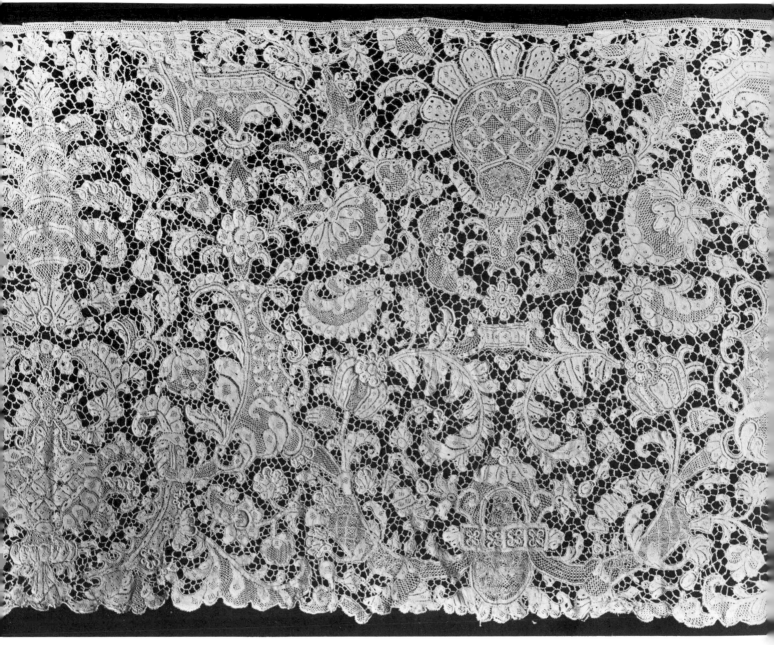

A beautiful balanced design which is close to those used by Daniel Marot for ironwork. The gates at Hampton Court, designed by Marot, can be seen to be in this tradition. He may have designed lace but there is no proof of it.
Victoria and Albert Museum.

A very fine piece of lace, made either for the King's own use or as a present for him to give. The luxury and idle fantasy of life at the court of Versailles are reflected here.
Victoria and Albert Museum.

ALENCON — Needle Lace

Alençon is a lace of which France is rightly proud. All through the centuries it has led French lace in design and quality. It was started in 1665 when in August of that year the town was given the exclusive privilege of making lace. Lace had been made there before then, but we know little about it. The workers were trained by Venetians and soon made the best lace. According to a manuscript from the Duke of Buccleuch's papers, Venetian lace was burned there in 1670 to show that Alençon lace was so good that the Venetian was no longer needed. From 1625 to 1675, Venetian lace led the world, then gradually France took over that position, led by Alençon. The Alençon designers introduced the use of bars without picots. These bars gradually became more neatly arranged until by 1700 a mesh ground had appeared. This ground was worked around the patterns from left to right. Gradually the mesh became straight and ran across the piece. Threads were laid to make a cordonnet or to make the centre of a leaf. These were then buttonholed over to make a hard crisp line. The pieces of the design were put together by yet another maker. When lace fell out of fashion at the end of the eighteenth century and muslin and soft fabrics were being worn instead of the stiff silks of the seventeenth century, many Alençon workers survived because the embroidery stitches used on white muslin were the same as many filling stitches. So when Napoleon wanted to revive lace making, he ordered lace from Alençon and there were workers to make it and to teach others. The French were slow to change, but by 1810 they were producing fashionable lace once again. Alençon went on to become a luxury lace of the nineteenth century. The cordonnet became more and more important as the ground became lighter and lighter so as to use less thread. At times the cordonnet was even worked over horsehair so as to make it hard and conspicuous. Finally, Alençon was most successfully made at Burano as table linen in the 1920s.

The earliest Alençon is indistinguishable from point de France. Colbert tried to control the designs of the lace made to his orders in the fourteen

Buttonholed Argentan bars, not a ground, on very early Alençon lace where the picots were dropped before anywhere else. A typical Alençon design. Width 2ins.

A superb piece of 18th century lace. Note the mirrored design.
The Metropolitan Museum of Art, bequest of Mrs. Jesse Seligman, 1910. (10.102.54)

Needle lace, 1700. This shows the very best that could be made at Alençon.
The Metropolitan Museum of Art, the Mabel Metcalfe Fahnestock Collection, gift of Ruth Fahnestock Schermerhorn and Faith Fahnestock, 1933. (33.90.145)

centres chosen by him for lace making. In this he failed and within ten years, by about 1675, different towns were making different laces. It is difficult to say that a piece of lace was certainly made in a particular town, but Alençon is the easiest to identify because Madame Despierre's book, *The History of Alençon*, written in 1886, is so comprehensive. Picots on bars were first dropped at Alençon and so pieces of lace, obviously early in design and without picots probably are from Alençon. When the bars became ground, a very fine ground indeed was used at Alençon; so fine that little of the lace has survived. The ground was changed to make it stronger by whipping the buttonhole mesh. This is the ground that is known as Alençon. A fine white thread was always used for French needle lace.

The tax free contracts that Colbert gave to the different lace centres only lasted ten years. During that time design, threads and workmanship were all controlled from Paris. After the end of the contracts, Colbert was unable to control lace making so rigidly, but the quality control did go on. After 1675, the various towns developed each in their own way. Alençon and Argentan, being only twenty miles apart, were probably under the control of the same manufacturers. Certainly they seem to have used much the same designs. The only real difference is in the grounds.

1680. This attempt to make the pheasant's eye stitch is interesting; or could it be a different stitch? Width 2ins.

The true pheasant's eye stitch with the whipped buttonhole ground.

Two pictures of the same piece of lace, showing how the maker used different filling stitches in each repeat of the design. The mesh is developed from bars, and is not a true ground. The heavy cordonnet and wide range of filling stitches make it Alençon, as do the points d'esprit or white dots, which were only used on the earliest lace.

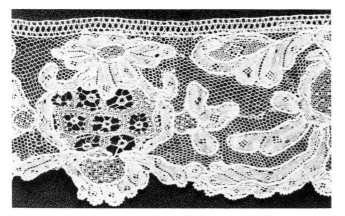

Whipped ground. Width 1¾ins.

A very early original looped buttonhole ground which was then whipped for strength. Width 2ins.

These two pieces of beautifully made lace were worked from almost the same ugly design.

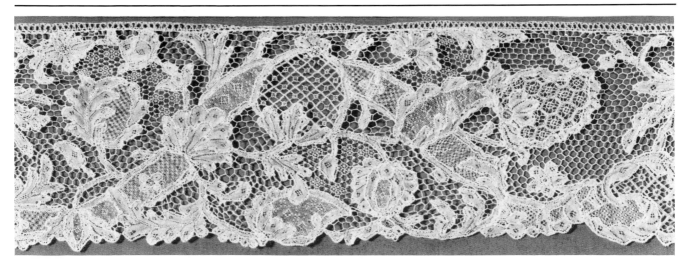

Needle lace, 18th century. A beautifully designed border using the same stitches as the preceding examples.

The Metropolitan Museum of Art, gift of Ann Payne Blumenthal, 1936. (36.130.35)

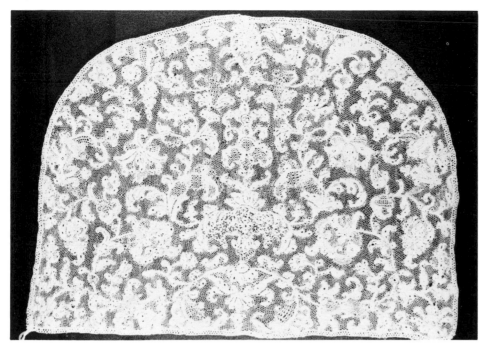

Cap back. A curious piece of needle lace. With its occasional raised edge, tightly buttonholed, and ground, it must be early Alençon.

Detail.

Below: Needle lace, 18th century. Louis XIV period. Note how the piece has been cut to form a shaped band.
The Metropolitan Museum of Art, bequest of Mrs. Anna Thalmann, 1934. (34.143.13)

Regrounded with later whipped Alençon ground. Width 2ins.

Right: 1710. The mesh is becoming more regular and the filling stitches are fewer. Width 2½ins.

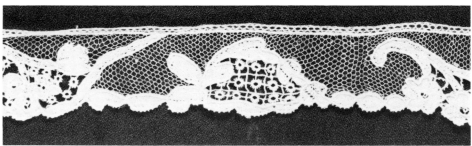

This very narrow piece shows control of the mesh and what became a standard filling stitch. Width ¾in.

Head-dress. Width 3½ to 7ins. The Metropolitan Museum of Art, gift of Mrs. Albert Blum, 1953. (53.162.23)

Right: 1720. In this much wider piece, the difficulty with the mesh still shows. Width 2½ins.

Width 1½ins.

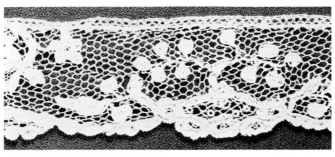

Width 1¼ins.

This wide 11½ins. border with a chinoiserie design shows all the best stitches used at Alençon and how beautifully they could be repeated to make a superb piece of lace. Blue and white china was very fashionable in the years 1730-40 and this lace of that date echoes that taste.

Needle lace, 1730.
The Metropolitan Museum of Art, bequest of Mrs. Jesse Seligman, 1910. (10.102.54)

Needle lace, 1730.
The Metropolitan Museum of Art, bequest of Catherine D. Wentworth, 1948. (48.187.602)

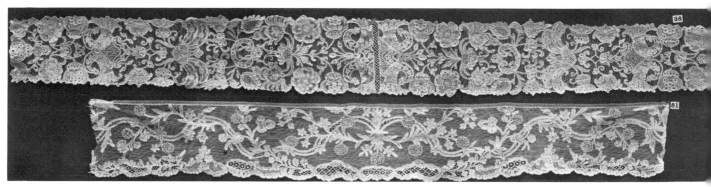

Two fine pieces, 1730. They show the beauty of the finest Alençon.
The Metropolitan Museum of Art, 1910. (10.102.77)

Needle lace, 1740. Border with dog and deer. Length 45ins., width 2¾ins.
The Metropolitan Museum of Art, gift of Mrs. Albert Blum, 1953. (53.162.39)

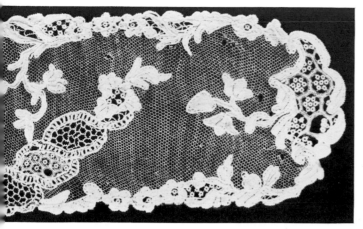

Lappet, 1740. This is of lesser quality than the chinoiserie piece. Width 3ins.

Lappet, 1740. The design is gradually moving outward. Width 3ins.

Cap back, 1750.
The Metropolitan Museum of Art, gift of Lady Reigate in memory of her mother
Mrs. William Redmond Cross, 1979. (1979.310.13d)

1750. The different sizes of the grounds give these two pieces a different appearance. Widths 2½ins. and 3ins.

1750. It is easy to see how fragile the original looped ground is. Width 1¾ins.

1730. Here the ground has been whipped. Width 1¾ins.

A contrast in grounds. It was early discovered that the original looped buttonholed ground did not last. This was then laced with extra thread to make the 'usual' Alençon ground. Much of it was regrounded in the 18th century, and most of the rest in the 19th. It is rare to find a piece with the fragile single ground.

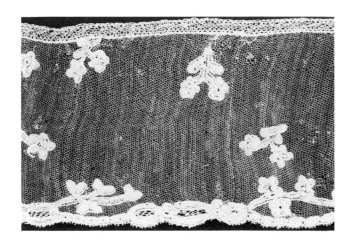 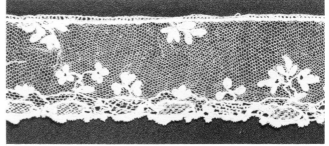

1760. A fine laced ground. Width 1½ins.

Left: 1760. Neither good workmanship nor design — a run of the mill lace. Width 3ins.

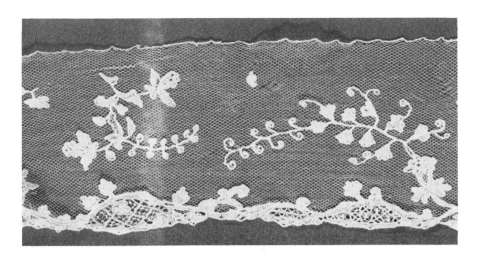

1760. Alençon motifs applied to Brussels bobbin ground. Width 3ins.

A beautiful design with top quality workmanship. The stiffly button-holed edges are becoming more conspicuous. Width 3ins.

Beautiful quality, if a somewhat confused design. Width 3ins.

99

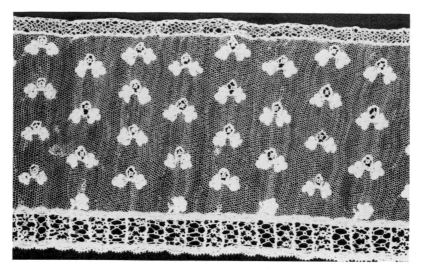

1775. Width 4ins.

Late 18th century lace, made just before disaster struck in the form of the French Revolution. Width 3½ins.

1775. Alençon applied to machine net. Width 1¾ins.

1780. An Alençon type design embroidered on machine net. Width 3ins.

100

ARGENTAN — Needle Lace

Argentan and Alençon lie twenty miles apart. Apparently both places had lace makers before 1665, so that they were ready to satisfy the French taste for handsome important lace derived from the Venetian tradition. The ground used at Argentan was hexagonal with ten buttonhole stitches worked over each side. This makes a tough looking heavy ground. Oddly, it does not wear well and much Argentan lace has been regrounded, either at Alençon or at Brussels, sometimes in the eighteenth century and often in the nineteenth century. Argentan is a crisp lace of great beauty, but it does not make good ruffles, and the softer grounds would have made it more fashionable. When the change in fashion to muslin came at the end of the seventeenth century, the Argentan lace masters were slow to change, but by 1720 they were once more amongst the leaders.

Argentan followed the fashions in design during the eighteenth century. Some time in the 1760s or 1770s the manufacturers of Alençon must have taken over the making of lace at Argentan, as the chief characteristics of Argentan fade out and into the Alençon traditions.

Argentella is a very finely made lace; it is really the best quality Argentan. The name 'Argentella' seems to have been invented by Mrs. Palliser, since there is no mention of it before the publication of her book.

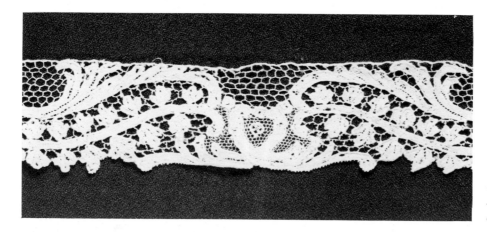

1680. Bars turning into mesh. Note the picoted bars behind the buds. Width 1in.

1690. Again the bars are not yet mesh. Each bar has been buttonholed. Width 2½ins.

Border, 1710. The central motif is of a cannon issuing smoke, reflecting the fashionable interest in the wars of Louis XIV. Length 21ins., width 5ins.

The Metropolitan Museum of Art, gift by subscription, 1909. (09.68.344)

This cap back is of outstanding design.

Detail showing the wide range of stitches.

1740. This rosace ground showing off the flowers is characteristic of 'Argentella'.
The Metropolitan Museum of Art, gift of Lady Reigate in memory of her mother,
Mrs. W. Redmond Cross. (1979.310.9)

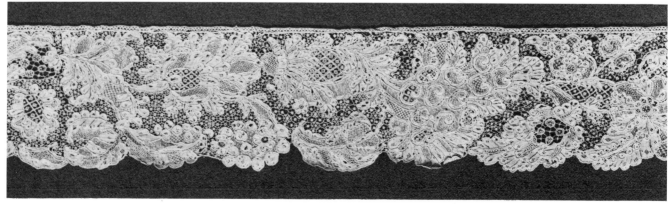

Needle lace, 1730. Another beautiful piece of the finest quality.
The Metropolitan Museum of Art, gift of Mrs. Edward L. Baylies, 1926. (26.18.8)

Needle lace, 18th century. Ecru cravat of medallions enclosing branches of flowers, with various grounds. Length 37ins., width 4ins.
The Metropolitan Museum of Art, gift of Mrs. Edward S. Harkness, 1930. (30.135.118)

1730. Section from a large and magnificent piece of lace. Width 10½ins.

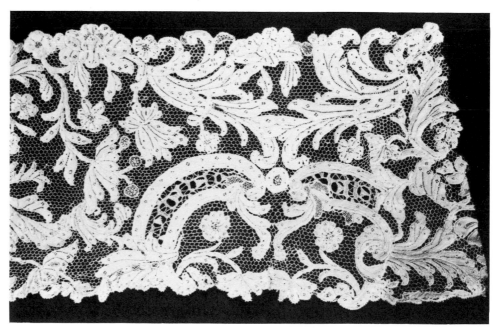

This detail shows the grandeur of the design

Needle lace, 1730. Strip with a design of foliated scrolls, hounds pursuing deer. So much French lace of the 1730s shows country scenes that one must believe that the rich courtly French loved the countryside more than the history books imply. Length 39ins., width 3¼ins.
The Metropolitan Museum of Art, gift by subscription, 1909. (09.68.346)

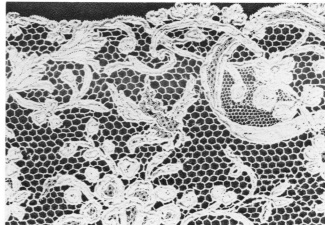

Lappet, 1740. This pretty and elegant lappet was clearly designed to be worn in a bow under the chin. Note the bird alighting on the bunch of flowers. The collector should beware of lappets made up by adding a narrow border to a wider one. In this case the design was meant for a lappet in spite of not being set at the usual angle. Width 3ins. The detail shows the ground clearly, and how badly it wears.

This beautiful border must have given great pleasure to its first owner.
The Metropolitan Museum of Art, gift of Mrs. Nuttall, 1908. (08.180.193)

Lappet, 1760. Width 3ins.

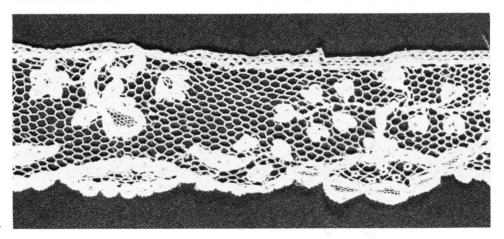

Width 1¼ ins.

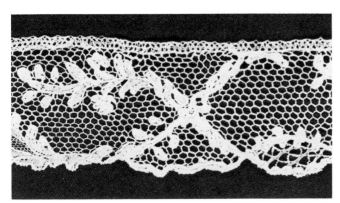

The ground has been repaired many times with buttonhole and whipping stitches. Width 1½ ins.

These designs are so like those of Alençon that only the Argentan ground identifies these pieces.

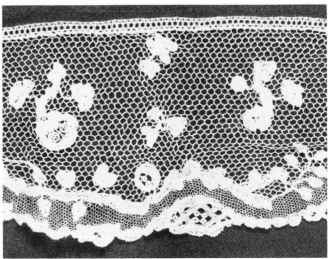

1760. Width 2½ ins.

CHANTILLY

Chantilly is near Paris. During the eighteenth century a great deal of lace was ordered from the factories there by the great ladies of the Court. When the revolution came, lace working was destroyed, but Chantilly lace had always been much admired, and copied, at Bayeux and Calais; from there Chantilly continued to be made for enormous export orders to Spain and the Americas.

Chantilly lace was made of dull black silk called grenadine, or of a pale blonde silk, or of white or black thread. It was a delicate fragile looking lace, with a fond chant (short for Chantilly) ground that is a six-pointed star ground or with a Lille ground with the motifs worked in a half-stitch or grille. The flowers are outlined with a heavy thread. During the third empire it again became the court lace. By 1860 it was widely copied in machine-made lace. The manufacturers answered this by producing even more and better designs and by using a joining stitch, called point de raccroc, so that many workers could be simultaneously making one big piece; thus an order for a big shawl could be completed in a few weeks, instead of a year. Nevertheless, by 1870 Chantilly handmade lace was a great luxury, made only for the few.

The machine-made copies of Chantilly are often finished by hand and it is very difficult to know where hand work begins and machine-work ends. The designs right up to 1900 were beautiful, with huge bunches of flowers or single flowers worked in different sizes for the different sized laces which made up a set. Wedding lace could be ordered, for instance, with everything necessary included and matching, even the lace for a fan. There is a beautiful set in the Victoria and Albert Museum made in 1890, which was never worn!

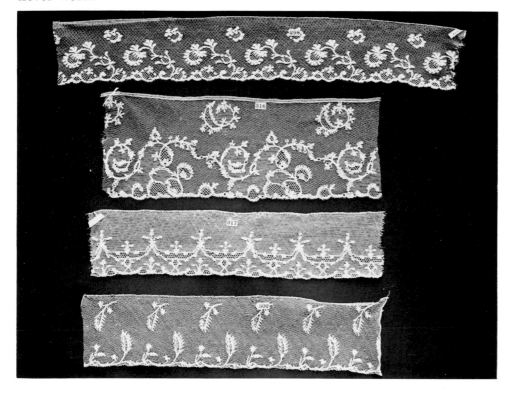

Chantilly white bobbin lace, 18th century.
The Metropolitan Museum of Art, gift of Mrs. Nuttall, 1908. (08.180.315)

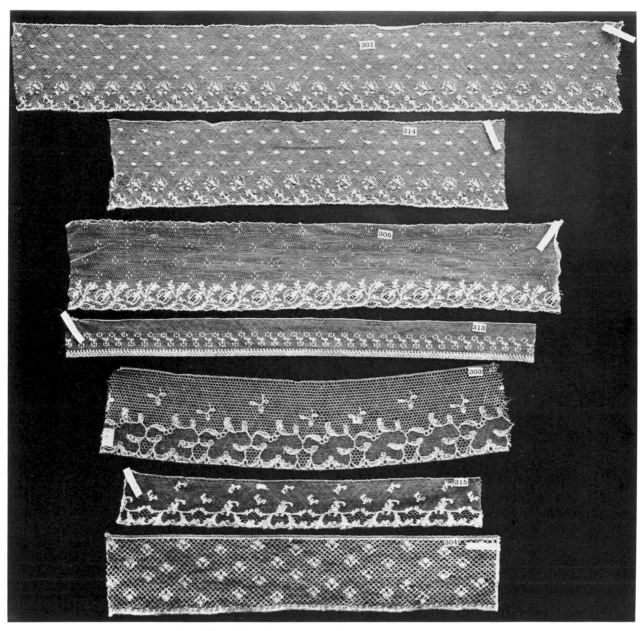

Chantilly white bobbin lace, 18th century.
The Metropolitan Museum of Art, gift of Mrs. Nuttall, 1908. (08.180.315)

LILLE

The first document to mention lace being made at Lille is dated 1582. It was then described as being identical to Arras lace (but we do not know what Arras lace was like!). Lille was the capital of Flanders until the treaty of 1668 when it became a French town. It soon became the second town of France. The designs were more Flemish than French. The lace is very like Mechlin with a thick thread outlining the design. There was always much use of square dots or points d'esprit, and the edges were straight. In 1803, when the price of thread rose, the ground was made coarser and lighter. Lille was a very light lace and made elegant ruffles. The ground is known as fond simple: it is hexagonal with two sides crossed and four sides twisted twice.

In March 1705, the lace masters of Lille asked for lower taxes from Paris. By 1723 the lace trade had so far recovered that there is no other mention of such a complaint. But in 1789 there were 18,000 workers, who, it was complained, had no work as a result of the revolution.

Lille was made well into the nineteenth century; a delicate lace, it was much beloved in hot weather.

When Heathcoat invented his net making machine in 1808, he made the net a copy of fond simple, or Lille or Bucks ground.

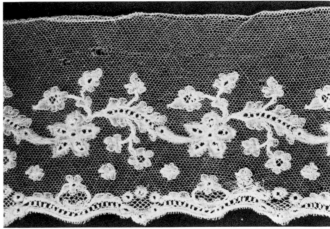

Above: 1760. Lovely leaves and a pretty edge. Width 4¼ ins.

Above left: 1750. A charming lace. Width 5ins.

A classical design of the 1760s. Note the birds pulling the chariot. Width 3½ins.

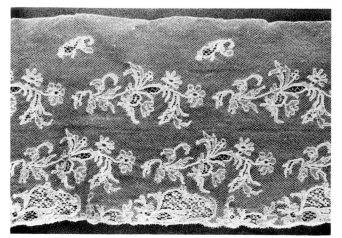 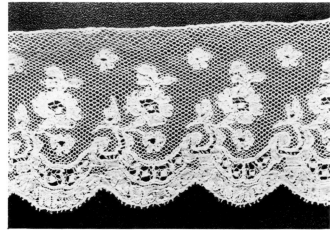

Two edgings, 1770. The Lille ground shows in both of them. Delightful lace was made in Lille at this period. Widths 5½ins. and 2¼ins.

A delicate piece of insertion. Width ¾in.

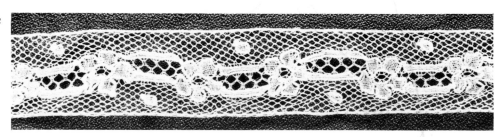

Insert, 1770. Width 1½ins.

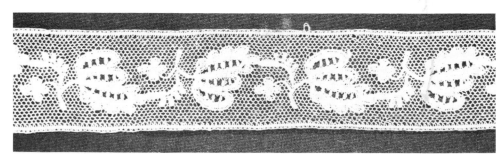

Edging, 1780. Width 3¼ins.

Edging, 1790. Width 2¼ins.

POINT DE SEDAN — Needle Lace

Point de Sedan is a most beautiful lace. It developed logically from the techniques and designs of Alençon and Argentan. We do not know where it was made. It does not seem likely that it was actually made at Sedan. There is not very much of it so perhaps it was made at Alençon to the design of one man or woman who originally came from Sedan. This is pure guesswork, but one of the great pleasures of lace collecting is that so little is known about so much that one can guess with a clear conscience! Wherever it came from and whoever made it, it has a distinct character of its own. The designs are beautiful and stately and the quality of the work is perfection. It must have been made at the turn of the eighteenth century. Madame Despierre, who wrote *The History of Alençon* in 1886 claims it firmly for Alençon on the grounds of technique. There seems no reason to doubt her argument; but it does not in fact prove anything.

It may well be that Alençon made 'Sedan' lace as its last fling at seventeenth century design. It was too handsome, too grand for the new clothes, so they switched to the delicate lace that we know as Alençon.

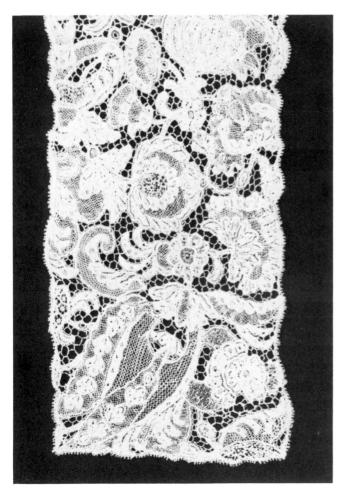

Square-ended lappet, 1700. The looped edge has been sewn on during the 19th century. Width 4ins.

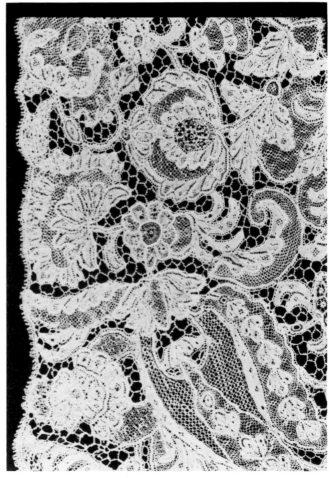

Detail shows the fine buttonholed edging on each piece of the design. The lace is heavy in looks and feel and could not compete with the new designs from Brussels.

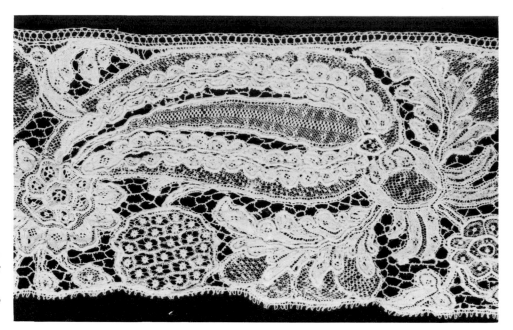

1700. A wonderful piece of lace. The details show the marvellous range of stitches used at this time. The whole repeat is too long to photograph. Width 2¾ ins.

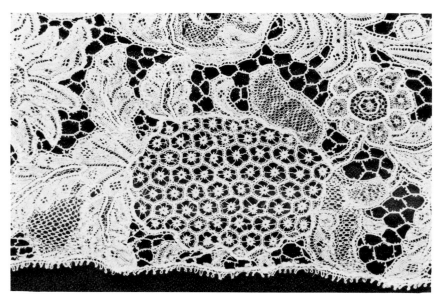

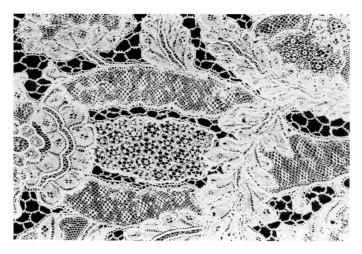

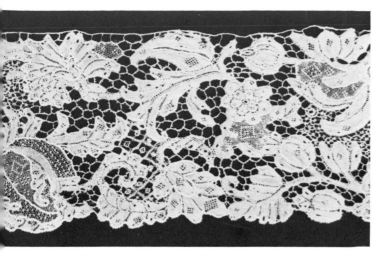

Two views of the same piece of lace as the repeat is so long. The superb design and workmanship are a joy. Width 3ins.

Width 2¼ins.

Collar.

Width 2½ins.

BINCHE AND VALENCIENNES — Bobbin Lace

Binche and Valenciennes lie thirty miles apart, a day's journey in the seventeenth century. Binche had a comparatively peaceful time in that century; Valenciennes on the other hand, was captured by Louis XIV in 1656 and was finally ceded to France in 1678. For twenty years, the poor people of Valenciennes had a miserable and uncertain time. Binche meanwhile was far enough from the scenes of war to develop a craft like lace making. Binche lace is, to our eyes, oddly balanced as the ground is always as important as the design. Valenciennes lace, however, always makes a clear distinction between design and ground. The designers appreciated silhouette. By the middle of the eighteenth century, Valenciennes had become one of the most popular laces in Europe, and the lace manufacture of Binche was absorbed by the manufacturers of Valenciennes. Valenciennes lace was made on an ever increasing scale and over a wider and wider area of France until by 1850 it was being made all across Northern France even including Normandy. The techniques were simplified and the designs beautiful. Valenciennes lace became the best loved of all laces, particularly as it must have been cheaper to buy than Alençon or Argentan and yet was as lovely.

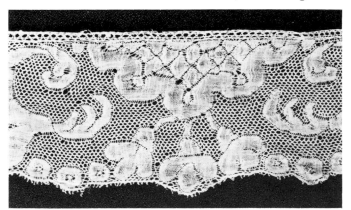
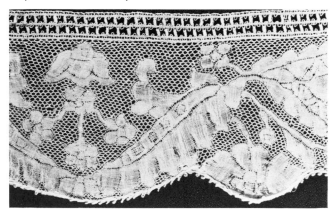

Two pieces of lace very close to Flemish designs of 1650. They both have the early round ground. Widths 1½ins. and 2ins.

Bobbin lace, 1710, Louis XIV period. Lappet with undulating design of flowers and leaves. The beautiful design is well balanced by the fond d'armure and round grounds. Length 23¼ins., width 13¾ins.

The Metropolitan Museum of Art, gift of Mrs. E.H. Simmons, 1935. (35.39.1)

1710. Lappet with beautifully balanced areas of quatre foil and cinq trous grounds. Width 4ins.

Edging, 1710. A curled leaf design with double grounds, cinq trous and fond d'armure meshes.

Binche and Valenciennes are both straight laces; the number of threads at the start is the same as the number of threads at the finish. It was not until about 1760 that extra threads were added to the designs in order to make the solids stand out even more against the ground. To save thread the square ground was used more and more.

Lace is still made at Binche, and Binche lace is still regarded as the finest of all lace. The Lace School at Bruges will not allow a student to learn Binche stitches until she has proved her expertise on the other Flemish laces, which include Valenciennes and Mechlin. The 'haloed snowball with a hole' is the best known of Binche stitches. It was also used at Valenciennes and Mechlin, but differently. The Binche stitches were worked diagonally, the Valenciennes and Mechlin stitches were usually worked either parallel with the edges or at right angles. The designs of Binche are very close to those of Valenciennes: without the aid of the French Government designers, one suspects that Binche workers may have 'pinched' some of the designs. Contemporary writers all refer to the wonderful Binche lace. In view of the popularity of Valenciennes and the immense amount of it made in so many places, it is not surprising that so many collectors of the beginning of this century did not appreciate Binche. The Lace School at Bruges has taught us all that appreciation.

The techniques of Binche are more complicated and difficult to work than those of Valenciennes. They are both really Flemish laces, but since Valenciennes has been part of France for more than three hundred years, must be included here.

1710. The cinq trous ground provides contrast with the solid designs. Width 2¾ins.

Edging, 18th century. A fine cinq trous ground balanced by quatre foil, fond d'armure and snowball fillings. Length 55ins., width 3ins.
The Metropolitan Museum of Art, the Mabel Metcalf Fahnestock Collection, gift of Ruth Fahnestock Schermerhorn and Faith Fahnestock, 1933. (33.90.155).

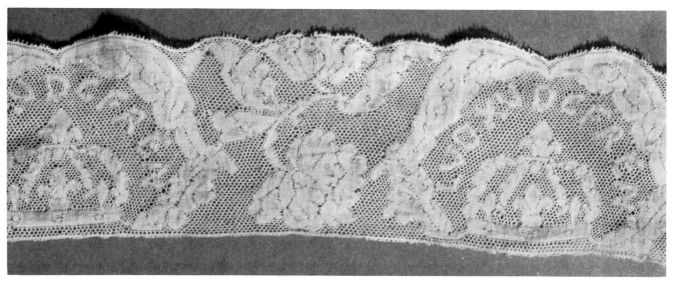

Bobbin lace, 18th century, sleeve ruffle. This lace, which is not of top quality, must mark the accession of Louis XV in 1715. The woodenness of the flower and the clumsiness of the lettering point to the same date.
The Metropolitan Museum of Art, Rogers Fund, 1936. (36.147)

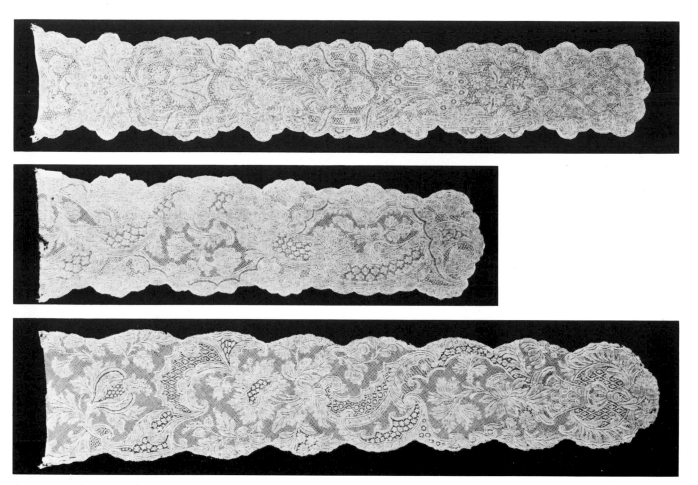

Lappets, 1720-40. The finest quality of Valenciennes lace that money could buy. When it was new every woman who saw it must have envied the owner. The designs are marvellous, echoing the silks of the dresses with which they were worn.

Victoria and Albert Museum.

A fine piece of lace with cinq trous ground. Width 2¾ins.

A mirrored design with a round ground and a 19th century footing. Width 1¾ins.

These pictures of lappets show the difference between the finest lace which would have been worn at court or at a very grand ball, and the good lace, such as was generally worn, illustrated in the two pictures immediately above.

Bobbin lace, 1730. Cravat (one of a pair). A lovely design, perfectly worked.
The Metropolitan Museum of Art, bequest of Mrs. Anna Thalmann, 1934. (34.143.3)

1720. A round ground. Width 1in.

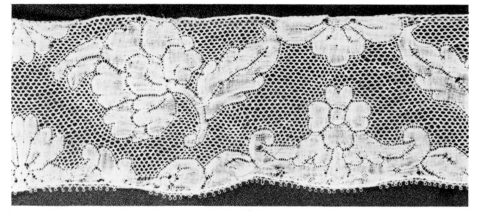

1730. A round ground, but with an edge coming in. Width 2ins.

Two handsome edges and lovely flowers on a pair of lappets.

Right: Bobbin lace, 1730. The design is of baroque bands enclosing conventional floral forms. Length 22ins, width 4ins.
The Metropolitan Museum of Art, gift by subscription, 1909. (09.68.258).

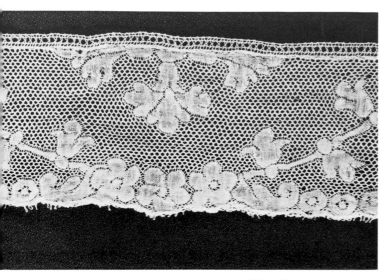

1740. Both these pieces have a round ground. Widths 1¾ins. and 2¼ins.

1750. Again, both have a round ground. Widths 1½ins. and 3ins.

Lappet, 1760. The design is thinner and the border more important than the centre. Width 3ins.

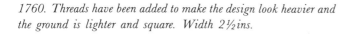

1760. Threads have been added to make the design look heavier and the ground is lighter and square. Width 2½ins.

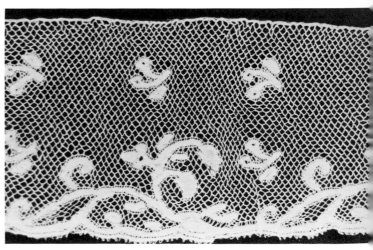

CHAPTER IV

Flanders

By the seventeenth century Flanders had been fought over so often that it is a matter of note that the northernmost area, the United Provinces, was at peace. A navy and a maritime empire were rapidly built up. By 1600 the people could afford luxuries, from fine paintings to lace. They were not interested in fashion, but dressed soberly in black, perhaps influenced by Spain, and throughout the century wore the same fine white lace with beautiful mirrored designs. No records of the making of this have been found, but when lace collecting became the fashion a hundred years ago, enormous amounts of this particular lace and no others, were found in the Netherlands. It is always called Dutch lace.

Further south lie Antwerp and Brussels. The women of Antwerp liked one design only to wear on their caps. This design, a pot of flowers with streaming leaves has been said to be a derivation from a design featuring Mary with two angels. This seems unlikely. For a century and a half this 'potten kant' design was worn.

Brussels had an elaborate system of guilds, particularly in the weaving trades. The machinery for setting up the making of a new textile, lace, was therefore comparatively easy, and Brussels lace masters soon organised a large business. The guilds were strict and any Brussels made lace always has quality. Cheaper lace was, of course, made but one always got what one paid for. In the province of Brabant, which surrounds Brussels, the guilds did not exercise the same control. Brabant lace, usually coarse and rather too light for its size, and not made of the best thread, shows up the advantages and disadvantages of the guild system. The designs of Brabant lace are good, just not very well worked, and the thread is poor, making it flimsy.

Both needle and bobbin laces were made in Flanders from the beginning. Lace, a new textile, was not hampered by tradition and in each place where it was made new techniques were experimented with. This is what makes early lace so fascinating to study — so many different solutions were found to the problems of lace making. In Flanders the best threads were available. Fine lace was made there very early in the seventeenth century and the stitches that show up fine thread were soon invented and put into use.

Further south again one comes to the area over which France and the allies fought again and again, where earlier Louis XIV had wanted more territory and the rest of Europe had tried to contain him. Straight laces were made at Mechlin and Valenciennes. Both places were fought over constantly. The seventeenth century generals and their armies fought according to an elaborate code of etiquette. Very few soldiers were killed or injured, but, since the soldiers took all the food they could find and then cut down everything else for fodder for their horses, the poor people living

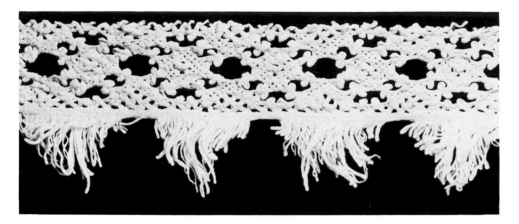

Bobbin lace, 2ins.

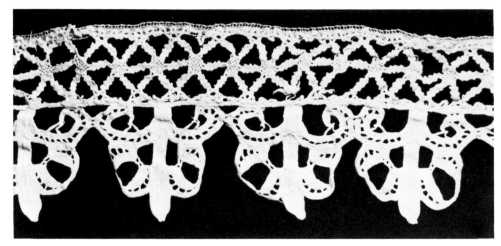

The bobbin insertion has a needle lace border of the same date. Width 2¼ ins.

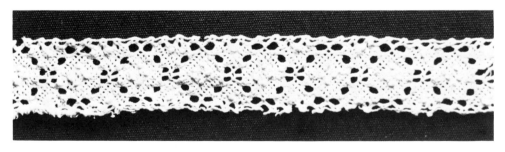

Bobbin lace. Width ⅝ in.

in the area starved. The Duke of Marlborough wrote home in 1709 of the poverty of the French peasants and of the horrors of their lives.

A great deal of lace was made in all areas of Flanders in the seventeenth century. It is interesting to try to see if a piece of lace could be an early example of Mechlin or Valenciennes. However, usually there is something to make one doubtful about putting a name; classification depends on technique only, as the brownish or white thread and designs show few distinctions.

Mechlin was called Malines by the French; point de Malines was the name used in England to describe Flemish lace. There was also a very fine white lace, mixed, which appeared at the end of the seventeenth century. This lace was called point d'Angleterre in France and point de Malines in

England. No one knows where this fine lace was made. Mrs. Palliser wrote that it was made in Brussels. Mrs. Jackson wrote that it was made in England. These two ladies were studying lace more than a hundred years ago, but we know no more than they did. Perhaps one day documents will be found to explain the puzzle.

In the eighteenth century all the towns made their own laces, and the different grounds make it easy to sort them. But once the high point of design and thread perfection had been reached about 1725, everything deteriorated. Lace was made lighter to save the cost of thread, fewer and fewer different stitches were used on each piece of lace, as that shortened the working times; finally the solid motifs almost disappeared and fashion took to muslin.

About 1800 the resurgence of demand for lace was coped with most intelligently in Flanders. Machine-made net was used as a base for embroidery, either by needle or with a hook, to make very pretty lace. There was also an increased demand for handmade lace. For the first thirty years of the nineteenth century, embroidered net supplied the cheaper

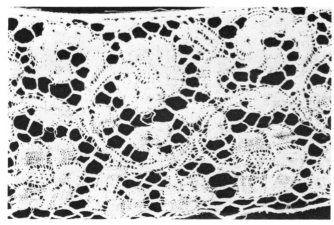

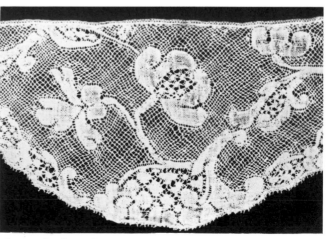

Bobbin lace, 1620. A Flemish copy of Genoese lace. Width 2¾ins.

Another Flemish piece that looks Italian. Width 3¼ins. Flemish lace was apparently made by many different hands. The threads of the ground needed, therefore, to be carried behind the motifs already made. Italian lace of this period did not need any threads to be carried as it was made all at the same time.

A very simple torchon ground. Width 4ins.

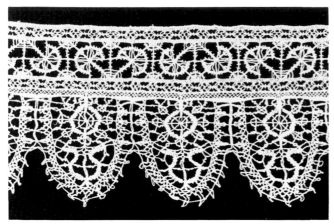

Needle lace border with bobbin lace scallops, 1600. Width 4ins. Compare this with the much larger collar worn by the Earl of Dorset in the portrait of 1613 (frontispiece). The thread is cream coloured and the lace feels hard like all needle lace, because buttonhole stitch is pulled so tightly.

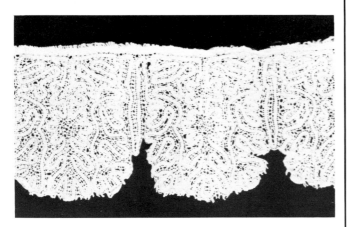

Bobbin lace, 1620. The design is obviously derived from the earlier one above. The lace is made of a very fine thread and feels soft. Width 2½ins.

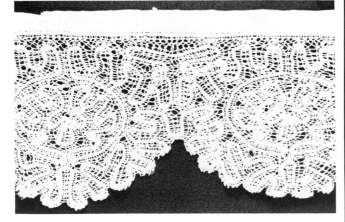

1630-40. The scallop is getting wider and wider. The design has clearly developed from the earlier ones. Width 4ins.

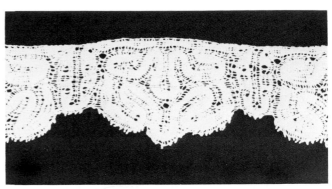

1630-40. A coarser version of the preceding one. The flattening scallops are smaller, showing the movement towards straight edged lace. Width 1½ins.

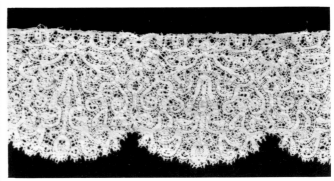

1630-40. The scallops are smaller again.
The Metropolitan Museum of Art, gift of Mrs. Nuttall, 1908. (08.180.156)

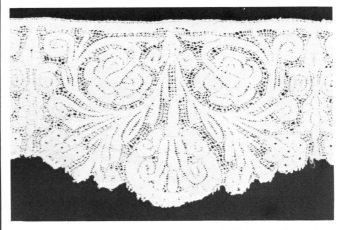

A flower is introduced. This piece is not wholly geometric, and an elementary mesh is shown. Width 3ins.

markets. Many engineers and inventors worked on lace making machines, and these appeared in commercially viable quantities by the middle of the century. Decorated net went out of fashion as the new machine-made lace gradually developed. In 1852, the Brussels manufacturers created a new and very fine handmade lace, point de gaze. This very beautiful and very expensive lace was an instant success because of its fine quality. Gradually machine-made lace took over the lace world, but even today it is possible to buy handmade lace in places like Bruges.

1640. A large flower head with the beginnings of a real ground. Width 2ins.

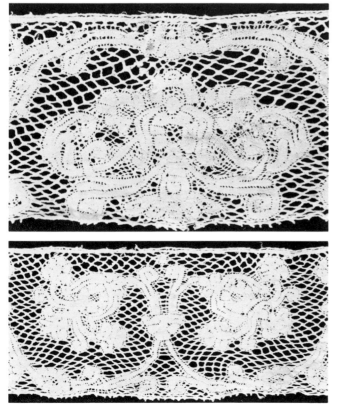

1650. Two views of the same piece with an unusual squarish ground with a thick crossing. There is a hint of an S scroll in the design. Width 2½ins.

1640-50. A little round mesh is showing, but it is really bars put in to hold the lace together. Width 2ins.

Here mesh can be seen developing, but it is irregular and untidy. Width 4½ins.

A real mesh is shown here. The design is still mirrored, but leaves are giving way to scrolls. Width 4ins.

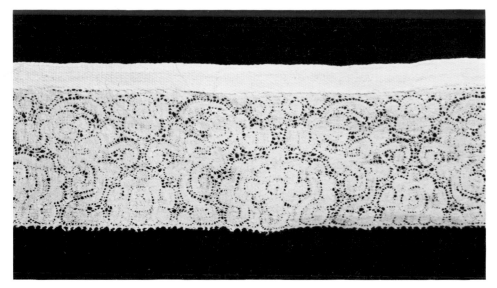

The pretty little edging widens the piece. The flowers and leaves are in a mirrored design, like all the earlier ones. Width 1½ ins.

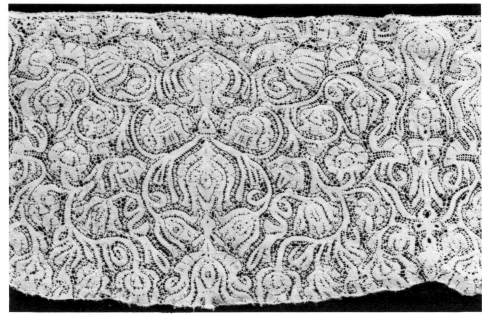

1630-40. Two examples with more complicated designs.
The Metropolitan Museum of Art, gift of Mrs. Nuttall, 1908. (08.180.156)

1650. A cinq trous ground. Width 3½ins.

A coarse piece showing a chalice, and candles. Width 2ins.

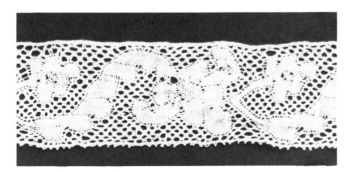

A narrow piece with a cinq trous ground. Width 1½ins.

The big flower head has become stylised and the scrolls are reverting to flower shapes. Cinq trous ground. Width 2ins.

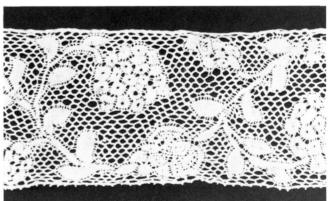

A round ground with the S scroll reappearing. Width 2½ins.

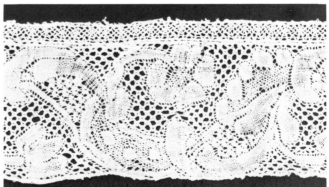

The scroll shapes now look like heavy leaves. The ground mixes cinq trous and fond de neige. Is this early Binche? Width 2ins.

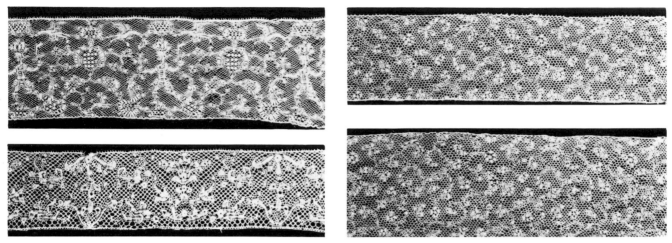

Bobbin lace, 1680-90. The piece top left shows a running figure bearing the orb. Length 18ins., width 1⅝ins.

The Metropolitan Museum of Art, gift of Mrs. Nuttall, 1908. (08.180.156)

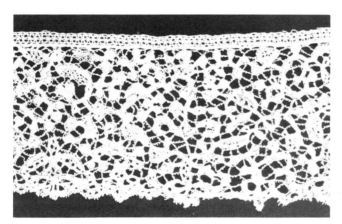

1690. This looks like an early Brussels lace. The design is much smaller and lighter and no mesh is to be seen. It looks like an attempt to copy point de France. Width 3ins.

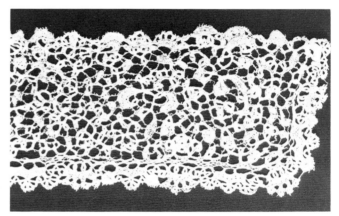

Collar, 1690. This, too, is a curious, chaotic design. Only the delicate edging is repetitive. Width 2½ins.

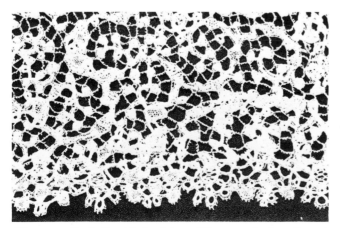

These are all similar kinds of lace. They may lead to Brussels bobbin lace in both design and technique. 9ins. square.

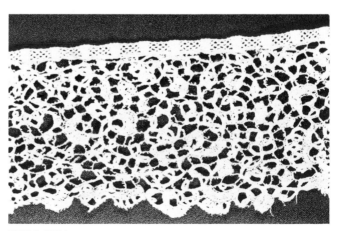

Width 2½ins.

The mesh is gradually developing, albeit tentatively. Width 10½ins.

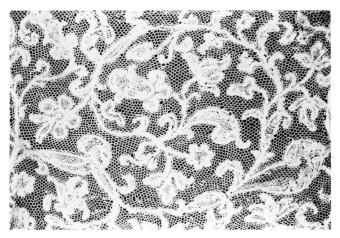

This is a joyous design — no mirrors here! Width 8½ins.

This again has an Italian influence. The ground is every which way. Width 10¼ins.

Detail showing the thread carried across the back of the design, proving it to be Flemish.

A wonderful piece. The quality of the workmanship and the fineness of the thread are clear. Width 20ins.
Private Collection.

Detail showing the back. The carried threads can be clearly seen, and the marvellous range of filling stitches.

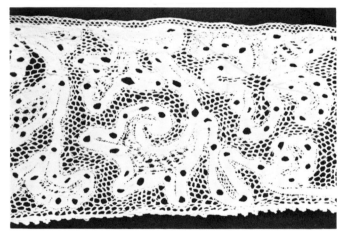

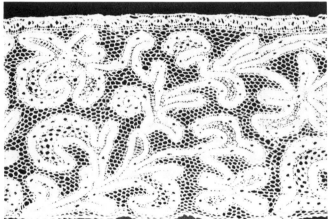

The Italian influence on the design is obvious. Width 3½ins.

The lace maker has greater control over the grounds. Width 5ins.

Note the fillings, the central decorated shapes in the design motifs, in this and the previous examples. The grounds are gradually becoming neater. Width 5ins.

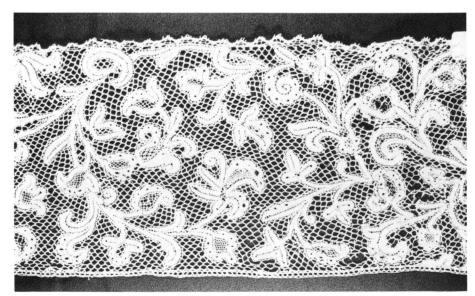

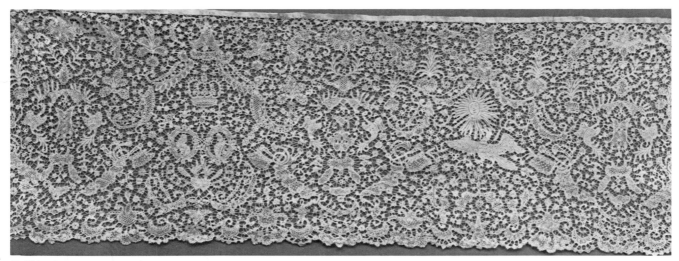

Bobbin lace, 1695. Flounce with medallion portraits of Maximilien Emmanuel and Therese Cunegond.

The Metropolitan Museum of Art, Rogers Fund, 1939. (39.107.2)

Bobbin lace, early 18th century. Two flounces, the top having vertical ornament of scrolls enclosing tulips and vase with leaves, the design connected by bars and the spaces filled by flowers and leaves. Length 3½yds., width 25ins.

The Metropolitan Museum of Art, gift of Mrs. Philip S. Van Rensselaer, in memory of Mrs. Tallmadge Van Rensselaer, 1909. (09.128.9).

A wonderful piece of bobbin lace, 1700, designed in the manner of Berain; an attempt to imitate French needle lace. Width 15½ins.

The detail shows the quality of the execution, with picoted bars and filling stitches imitating needle lace.

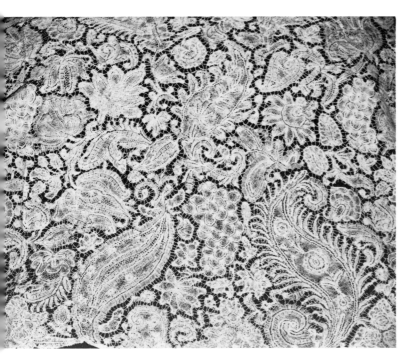

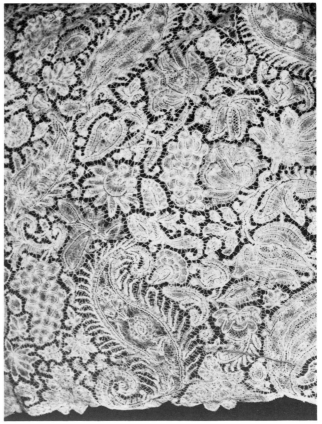

This handsome, wide piece of bobbin lace, 1710, is more in the Sedan tradition than the preceding piece. It has an interesting design with bunches of grapes and recognisable garden flowers. Width 21ins.

These designs of 1710 are copies of needle lace made by joining twisting tapes of bobbin lace with needle lace stitches. In this example the elaborate twisting tape design is as busy as any French needle lace. Width 13½ ins.

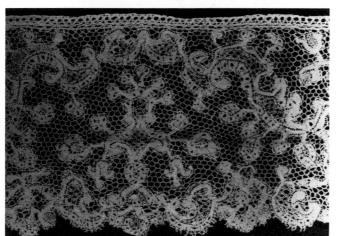

Width 2¾ ins.

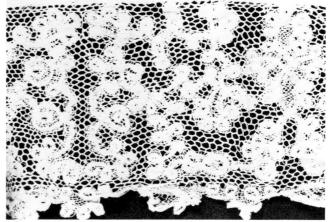

Width 4ins.

This piece of twisting tape lace has pretty filling stitches. Width 10ins.

1720. Very fine brownish thread was used for these pieces. The various stitches are beautifully worked but the grounds are not neatly carried out. Width 16½ins.

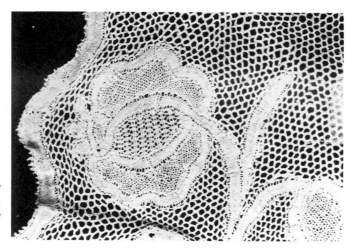

Detail. The outer sections of the persimmon worked in half stitch are highlighted by the central section in fond de neige.

Width 6½ins.

134

1760. A circular piece of lace for the bottom of an alb. The technique is Flemish, but the design of the wreath comes from the book by the architect Guarino Guarini of Turin. This could have been ordered for the Spanish market. Width 15½ins.

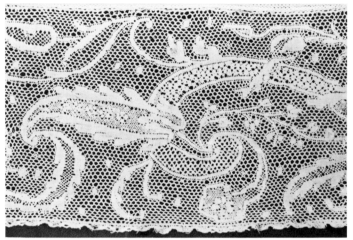

1740. A lovely piece though not of the finest quality. Width 5ins.

A beautiful design, well carried out. Width 7½ins

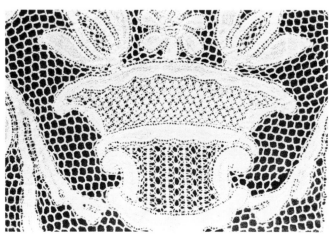

Detail showing the fine stitchery.

ANTWERP

Flemish conservatism is shown in the long lasting design of potten kant which was worn by the women of Antwerp for a century and a half from about 1630. Its origins are lost, but it is hard to believe the tradition that the rigid pair of flowers ever derived from angels.

1725. Potten kant design. Width 5¼ins.

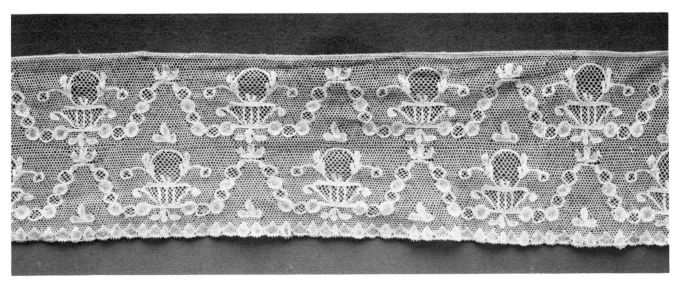

Bobbin lace, 1750. A potten kant border with two rows of flower pots and running chains.
The Metropolitan Museum of Art, gift of Mrs. Dean Sage, 1910. (10.21.7)

BINCHE

Binche is technically the most difficult of all bobbin laces to make. It is the supreme lace made in the Flemish tradition. Binche lies in Belgium and even today, fine lace is made there and is taught at Bruges. Valenciennes lace is also in the Flemish tradition, but it must be considered a French lace as it has been in France for more than three hundred years.

Binche did not develop, as Valenciennes did, into a popular lace. It was always too beautifully made and therefore too expensive. The French organized Valenciennes lace so that it could be quickly and neatly made. It became a very popular lace and was made in many places as well as in Valenciennes. In the nineteenth century, it was made all over Northern France and sold well long after other sorts of lace had disappeared.

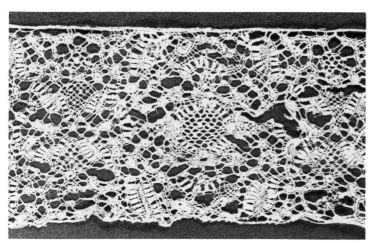

1660. This Flemish lace is generally considered to be the earliest type of Binche. Width 2½ins.

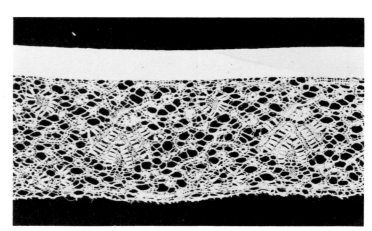

The thicker patches are in the shape of coats of arms. This example comes from the famous Macleod Collection of Flemish lace. Width 1¾ins.

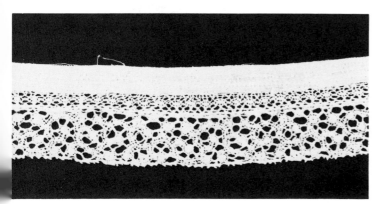

1660. An early piece with no mesh. The joined bars make it difficult to see the wiggly design. Width 1in.

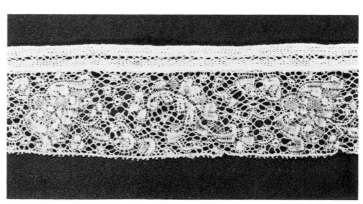

Here the flowers and the Binche feathers can be made out. There is no mesh; instead haloed snowballs with holes — a Binche ground. Width 1in.

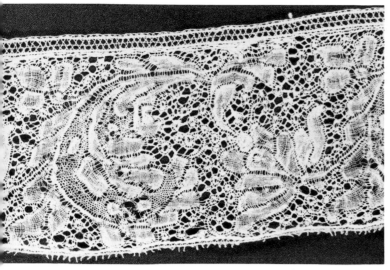

A large design, but the same mesh can be seen in the same ground. Width 2¾ins.

A 19th century footing has been added. Here the ground has really taken shape, but it is still the same stitch. Width 2¾ins.

1690. All these pieces have the well known Binche stitch of haloed snowballs with holes.

1690. The beautiful snowball ground shows up the design. Width 1½ins.

Fond de neige can be seen here, with the snowball ground. Width 1in.

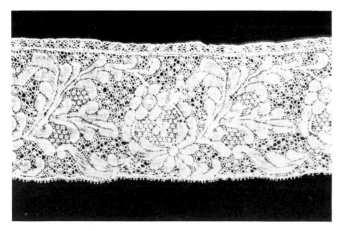
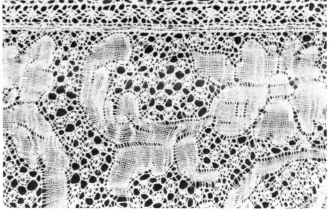

The same typical combinations of snowball ground and fond de neige fillings. Width 2¾ins.

Detail showing the stitches: snowball and whole stitch, and the neat holes that outline each piece.

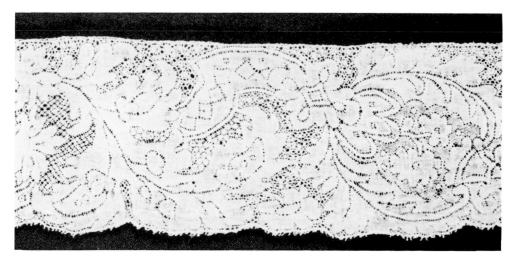

Note the snowball, fond de neige and whole stitches lightened by tiny bars, like point d'Angleterre. Width 2ins.

Flemish, not Binche. Compare the stitchery in the illustrations above. No snowballs of any sort, only the easy cinq trous ground and ordinary whole and half stitch. Width 2¾ins.

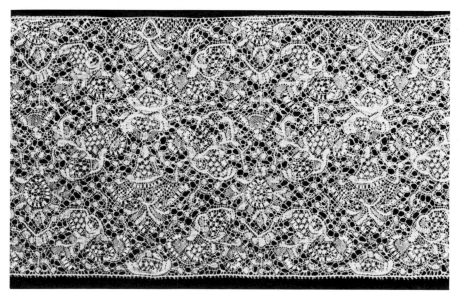

1700. A wide and fine piece of early Binche showing all the early types of design and stitchery. Notice the ground of haloed snowballs and the many small white points d'esprits. The irregular holes are also characteristic of Binche lace. This is a lace which is technically very difficult to make.

Above: 1700. The snowball and fond de neige grounds show up the design. Width 2¾ ins.

Above right: Two narrow pieces sewn together to make a cheaper lappet. Width 2¾ ins.

Right: The end of a lappet. The design of flowers stands out clearly. Note the fine snowballs.

Binche lace made soon after 1800. Binche of this date is very rare. It looks like Valenciennes and is often mistaken for it, but the Binche technique is there, with its own stitches.

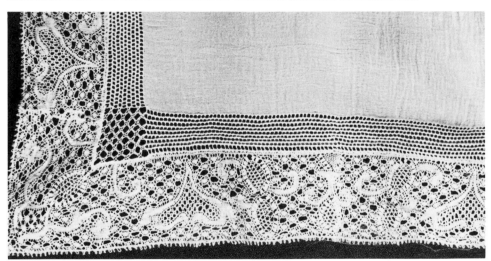

Border 1in. wide on a handkerchief 8ins. square.

2ins. at the widest point.

BRUSSELS

It is not known when Brussels lace was first made. It is said that there is gothic lace in some of the Brabant churches, apparently of the fifteenth century. Lace in Brussels has always been made both by needle and by bobbin. In both cases, the ornaments were made first and the grounds added later. Needle made ground started about 1660 but lace with the ornaments joined by bars continued to be made until 1750. The needle lace ground was made by a single thread in a single loop. It was very fragile, light and pretty and cost three times as much as the bobbin ground. The bobbin ground was hexagonal with four sides twisted and two sides plaited. This ground is sometimes called droschel. The cordonnet is not buttonholed but is a bundle of threads evenly stitched into place.

In the late seventeenth century, the Brussels lace copied the point de France and some very pretty chinoiserie designs were made at the beginning of the eighteenth century.

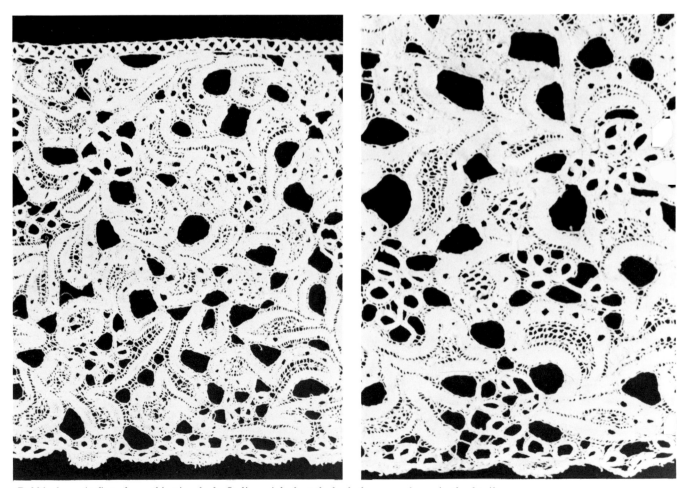

Bobbin lace. At first glance this piece looks Italian. A look at the back, however, shown in the detail on the right, shows the looped threads that prove it to be Flemish. The twisted loops of what looks like narrow tape are typical of early Brussels lace. Width 7ins.

Needle Lace. Eighteenth century Brussels needlepoint lace is very beautiful. The designs are fabulous, with scalloped borders. The repeats are very long, many are twenty inches; the ground is worked after the decorations and is absolutely straight showing up the curves and richness of the design. The cordonnet is lightly buttonholed, many different stitches are used on the ornaments, and many elaborate grounds join them together. Later, needle lace ornaments were sewn to bobbin grounds.

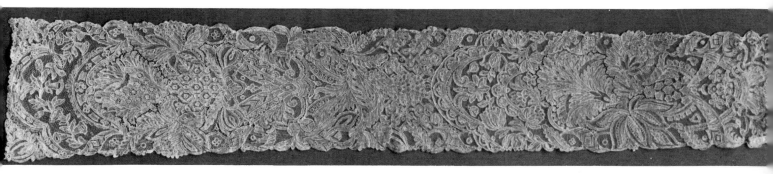

Needle lace, 18th century. A marvellous lappet; the beauty of the design is matched by the delicate working.
The Metropolitan Museum of Art, Rogers Fund, 1939. (39.107.6)

Needle lace, 1710. A fine piece of Brussels lace with a mirrored design.
Victoria and Albert Museum.

Needle lace, 1720. A beautiful piece of lace with its flamboyant design elegantly balanced.
Victoria and Albert Museum

142

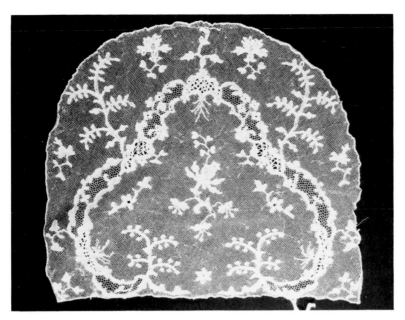

Needle lace held together by a bobbin ground, 1750.

Needle lace, 1750. Alençon on Brussels grounds. Width 3ins.

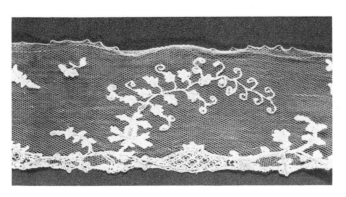

Needle lace, 1750. Width 3ins.

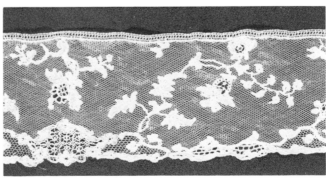

Needle lace on bobbin ground, 1750. Width 1½ins.

Bobbin Lace. During the eighteenth century, the bobbin lace had pretty, naturalistic flowers elegantly arranged with ribbons. As the century moved on the designs became lighter, as more ruffles were worn. Gradually classical designs came in, and then the edges of the lace became all important with rows of pretty leaves or flowers and spots on the background. The Brussels lace masters were always clever, and the lace became lighter as the price of thread rose, and the designs changed with every breath of fashion. In the middle of the nineteenth century a new lace was started, called point de gaze. This very pretty elaborate lace had flowers with raised petals and tight overall patterns. It was made both of needle and bobbin lace. Lace is still made in the environs of Brussels.

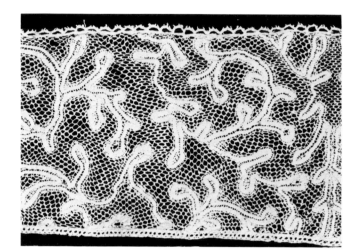 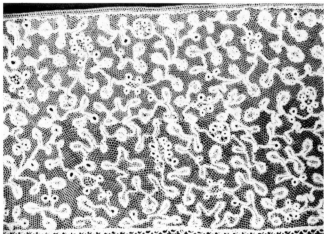

1680. Two examples of the early use of Brussels ground. Widths 3¾ins. and 7ins.

Towards the end of the seventeenth century, Brussels lace became distinguishable from other Flemish laces. It was made by quite a different method. The making of Brussels lace was organized in separate repeated tasks as is the making of a car. A master planned the lace and handed out the patterns and threads. The basic motifs were made by one woman, the elaborate centres by another, they were then joined together by another, and so on. The most elaborate pieces took anything up to twenty-two different steps and twenty-two different workers. One result of this method is that the Brussels ground for the first half of the eighteenth century was made to flow about the design, the ground worker fitting the stitches around the motifs. The other Flemish laces being made by one person in one piece had neat tidy rows of ground. The Brussels workers copied their rivals and finally made the grounds straight. To begin with, Brussels lace was made with bars, which even had imitation picots. According to Mrs. Palliser, and she gives no reference for the statement, bars were given up in 1762. Gradually the lace became lighter with more ground and fewer solid patterns. By 1800, only the edge had patterns and the soft delicate ground, which fell so beautifully, gave the lace its character.

In the nineteenth century, vast quantities of lace were made. Motifs of both needle and bobbin lace were sewn onto both handmade and machine-made nets. Many old designs were copied. The copies of gros point de Venise are magnificent in their workmanship, but the designs are rigid and the thread a distinct shade of ecru. The beautiful point de gaze was very successful as a new lace. It was of course very expensive, but it was so distinctive and magnificent that it was bought.

Lappet, 1690. This lovely lace looks like embroidered muslin. The scalloped edge and round daisy like flowers are typical Brussels designs. Width 3ins.

Bobbin lace cap back, 1710. This piece has very little ground.

Bobbin lace, 1700. This shows the beginning of mesh grounds. Width 2¾ins.

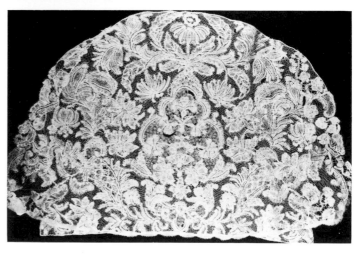

Collar, 1710. The mesh gradually became straighter and neater.

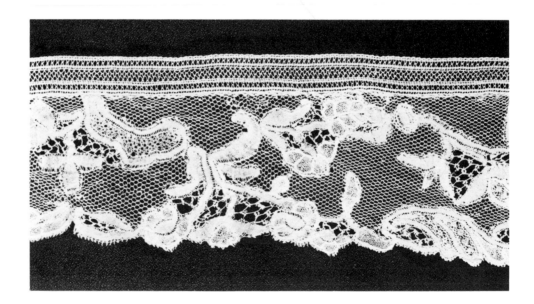

Width 1¾ ins.

Width 1¾ ins.

Bobbin lace, 1710. The ground in this collar is not sufficiently controlled.

The ground here is still worked around the design. Width 2¾ins.

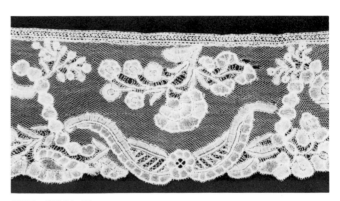

1710. 18ins. repeat; width 3ins.

1730. Width 3ins.

Two pieces of bobbin lace worked to the same design, but a number of years apart. The ground of the first piece has been worked around the design, but that of the second has been worked with a straight mesh. Both are, of course, Brussels mesh.

1710. This mesh is already true Brussels mesh, but the technique has not quite been mastered. Width 2½ins.

Lappet, 1720. Here the mesh is tidier than in the border to the left but is still not straight. Width 3¼ins.

This superb piece of lace would have been sewn flat onto a fine silk for an important dress. The ground is still not under control, so it dates from 1720. Width 8½ ins.

This detail shows the quality of the workmanship. The stitches are arranged to give light and shade to the design. It is not black and white but varies in tone.

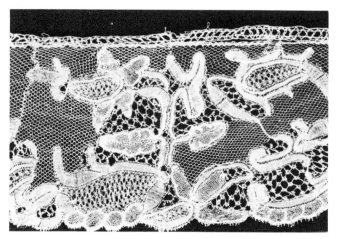

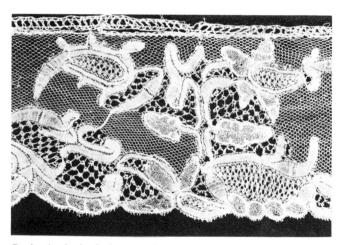

Front. Even at the front one can see the carried threads.

Back. At the back they are clear to see.

Many miles of these delicate pretty edgings were made in the early 18th century. Width 2½ ins.

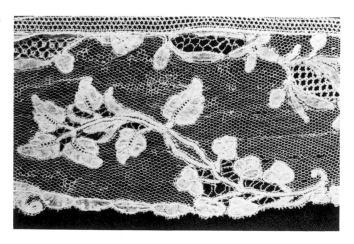

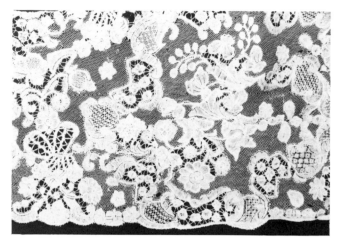

An unsatisfactory piece of 1740-50. The design is elaborate but one's eye cannot settle. The workmanship is slapdash. The ground goes every which way. Cut to 6ins.

1740. Fragment of an elegant design, beautifully worked, in great contrast to the piece to the left.

Bobbin lace border, 1740. Width 2½ins.

Detail, showing how the ground joins the design, and the fine balance of different stitches.

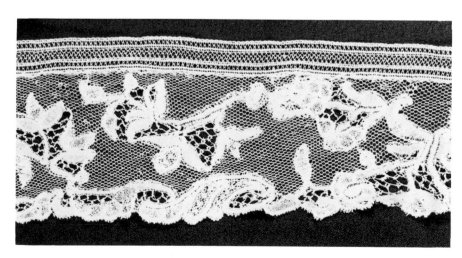

A lovely edging. Width 2ins.

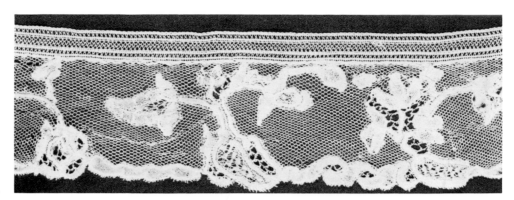

Bobbin lace, 1750. Width 1¾ ins.

Bobbin lace, 1750.

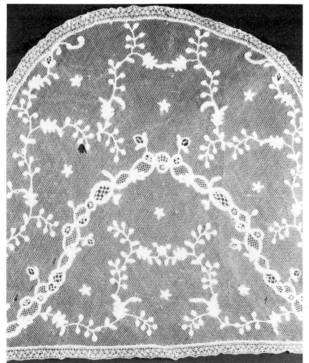

Cap back with matching lappet, 1770. The cap back is much more worn than the lappet.

Bobbin lace, 1780. Width 2¾ ins.

Needle lace applied to a bobbin ground, 1780. Width 2ins.

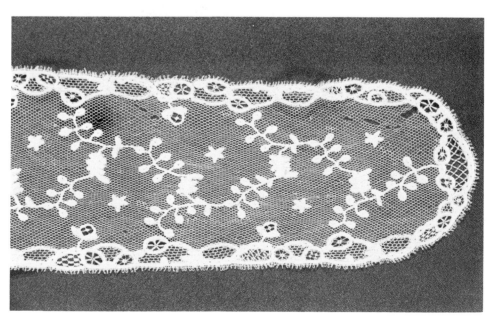

Bobbin lace applied to a bobbin ground, 1780. Width 3¼ins.

1770. A very pretty delicate border. Width 2½ ins.

1770. The narrow strips that make up the ground are clear to see. Width 9ins.

1770. Mixed lace applied to machine net. Width 5ins.

This piece shows the strips in the bobbin ground. The strips were sewn together with a special stitch and can just be seen. Width 10½ ins.

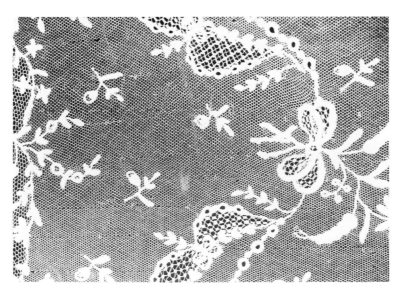

BRABANT

Brussels is in the province of Brabant. There is a rather flimsy lace, large in size and design, which is called Brabant lace. It is obviously a furnishing lace, too large for any dress. The designs link up with Brussels designs in taste. Presumably this lace was made in the countryside near Brussels and was not made to the orders of the lace masters of Brussels. The quality is not up to Brussels standards.

1720. The designs are good, but the thread is not first class, nor is the workmanship. Width 11ins and cut.

1730. Slightly later, with an added border. Width 8ins.

1740. A beautiful design but very badly carried out. Width 8½ins.

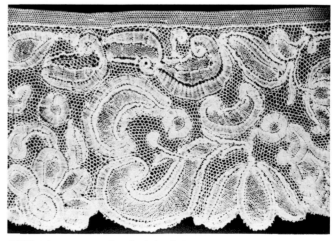

1760. A very poor piece both in design and workmanship. Width 6ins.

MECHLIN — Bobbin Lace

Before 1665, all Flemish lace was called point de Malines — Malines being then in France. When Louis XIV lost Flanders, Malines became Mechlin, but in England all Flemish lace was called point de Malines until about 1700. In 1699, the act prohibiting the sale of foreign lace (except French lace) in England was repealed and enormous amounts of it were sold.

Mechlin was the first lace centre to have its name used, beginning in about 1650. At that time needle lace was dominating the lace world, and it was 1700 before the fine delicate lace made by bobbins was really appreciated. The firm thick thread of Mechlin strengthened the very light ground and made it the ideal lace for ruffles. There was a very big Beguinage, or almshouse, in Mechlin. There large quantities of the lace were made under careful supervision. Thus the quality was kept to a high standard. Queen Anne paid nearly three pounds a yard for eighty-three yards of Mechlin for her Coronation. In 1713, the total cost was £247.6.9 and this would have to be multiplied by fifty or sixty to compare with today's money.

Mechlin is a straight lace and can only be distinguished from Valenciennes made in the seventeenth and eighteenth centuries by the heavier thread used as a cordonnet which was always used in this lace. The early grounds were very beautiful.

1675. A very fine, very early piece. The ground is made of different filling stitches. The quality is superb. Width 2ins.

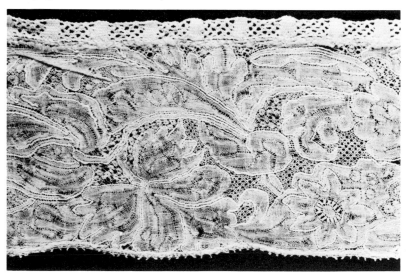

1680. A snowball ground. The design of the leaves is beautiful. Note the haloed snowballs with holes, as used at this time at Binche. The heavy thread identifies this piece as Mechlin. Width 1¾ins.

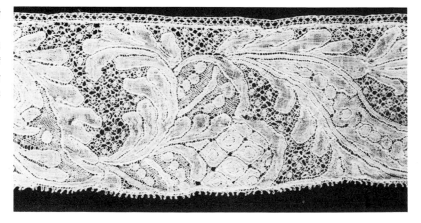

A strange design with a mixed ground of fond de neige and snowballs. Width 2¼ins.

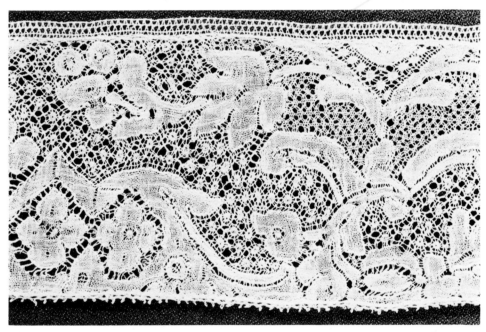

Detail.

A lovely design using the same mixture of stitches. Width 1½ins.

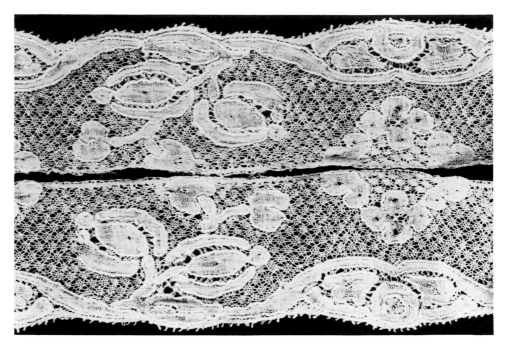

These pieces were made to be sewn together to form a lappet: in contrast to many Mechlin pieces, a coarse design. Width 1¼ins.

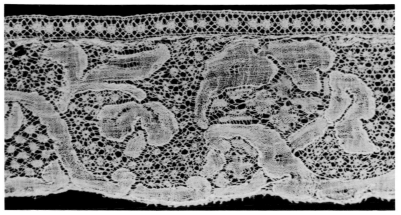

1690. A handsome piece with its snowball ground. Note the thick Mechlin thread, used nowhere else. The thick thread is the same back and front, in fact there is no wrong side. Width 2ins.

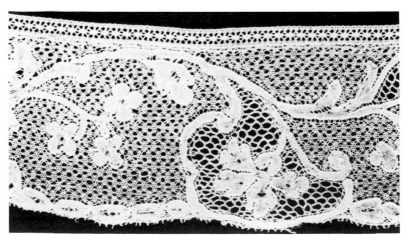

A piece with fond d'armure ground. Width 2ins.

Enlarged detail. Mechlin, ground fond d'armure. Length 43ins., width 3½ins.
The Metropolitan Museum of Art, gift by subscription, 1909. (09.68.238)

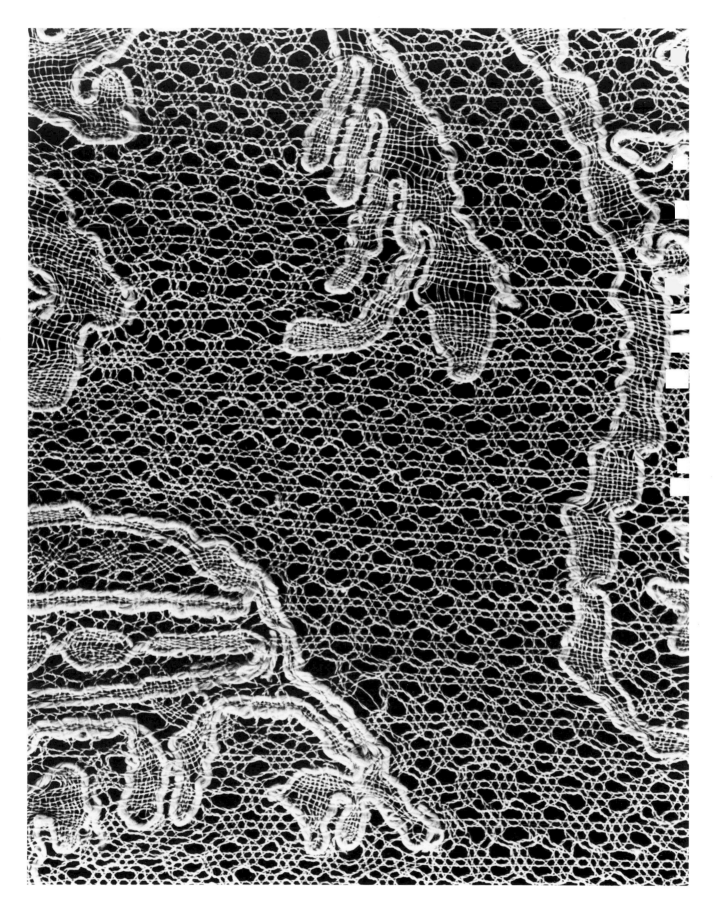

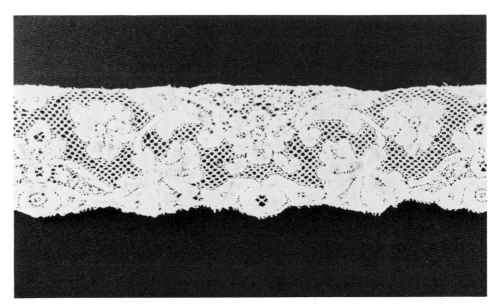

1700. An early piece with a mirrored design and a cinq trous ground. Width 1¾ins.

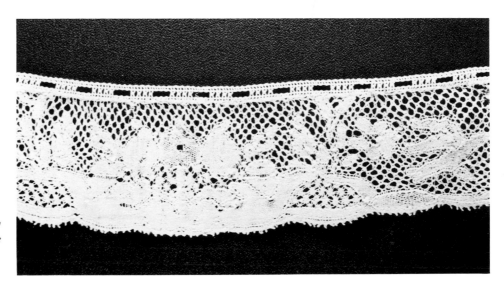

Note the bird (which is balanced by another flying in the opposite direction). Cinq trous ground. Width 1¾ins.

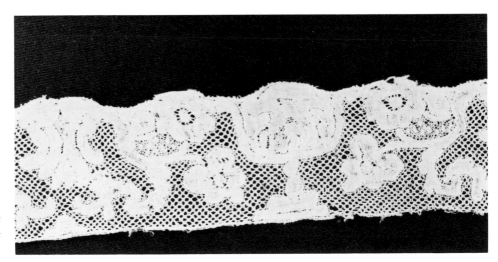

An early church piece with its chalice design mirrored, cinq trous ground. Width 2ins.

1710. Another mirrored design but with a fond de neige ground. Width 1¾ins.

A cinq trous ground, balanced by a fond de neige ground. The design is no longer mirrored. Width 1¾ins.

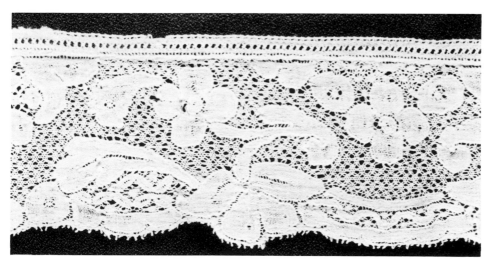

1720. A solid fond de neige ground. Width 1¾ins.

Lappet, 18th century. Length 49ins., width 3ins.
The Metropolitan Museum of Art, gift by subscription, 1909. (09.68.248)

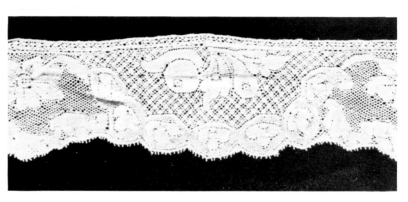

1710. A beautiful, very fine piece with a plaid ground well balanced with the Mechlin ground. Width 1½ins.

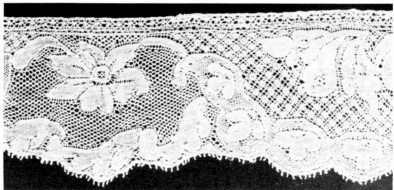

Detail, showing the fineness of the stitchery and the elegance of the half stitch petal background behind the whole stitch buds.

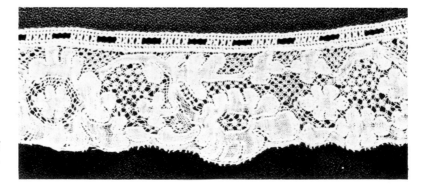

1720. Here snowflakes and cinq trous are beautifully balanced. Width 1¼ins.

1730. *The lovely rococo shield shape was much used at Mechlin. The tulip is well balanced by the grapes. Width 1½ ins.*

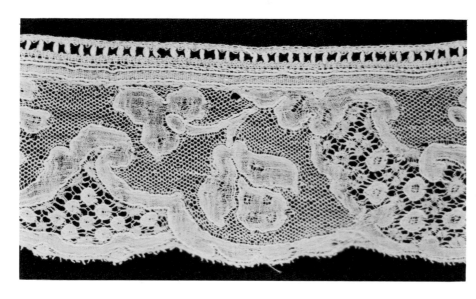

Detail, showing how well the grounds balance. The petals are lightened by stars in squares.

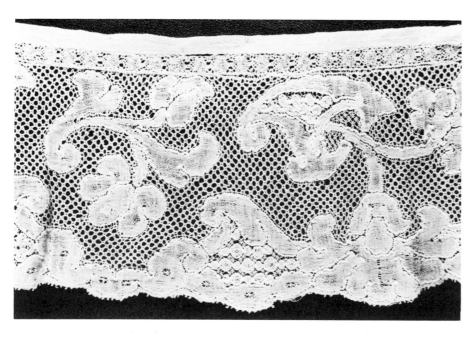

Another way of using shield shapes, this time balanced by a carnation. Width 3½ ins.

Bobbin lace border, 18th century. A ship design.
The Metropolitan Museum of Art, gift of Mrs. Albert Blum, 1953. (53.162.35)

Bobbin lace, 18th century. Border of basket of flowers alternating with huntsman and reindeer. Length 54ins., width 1½ins.
The Metropolitan Museum of Art, gift by subscription, 1909. (09.68.253)

1740. The Mechlin ground in full use balanced by quatre foil. Width 1¾ins.

Another pretty piece of insertion lace. Width 1in.

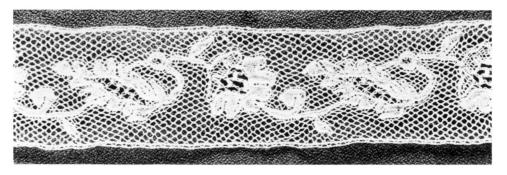

Cap back of Mechlin bobbin lace, 1750. The design is of Orpheus with his lyre.
The Metropolitan Museum of Art, gift of Mrs. Edward S. Harkness, 1930. (30.135.130)

1740. Here chrysanthemum leaves balance a tulip. Width 1¾ins.

1760. A 19th century footing has been added. Width 2¼ins.

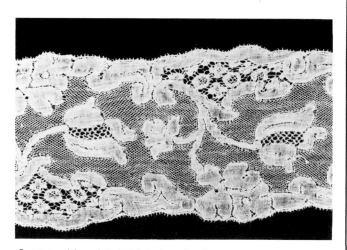

Lappet with a delightful design of tulips.

1770. This lappet is in very bad order, but it shows how the design is moving outwards. Width 3ins.

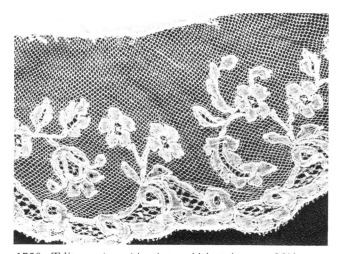

1750. Tulips again, with what could be primroses. 2¾ins.

This piece is in better condition and the stitchery can be seen more clearly.

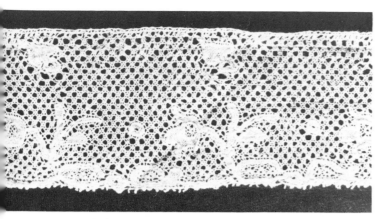

1780. A cinq trous ground. Width 2ins.

1790. The straight edge with a curly design and rows of tiny hanging threads date this piece and the one below. Width 1½ins.

Width 2¾ins.

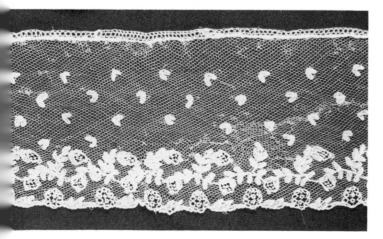

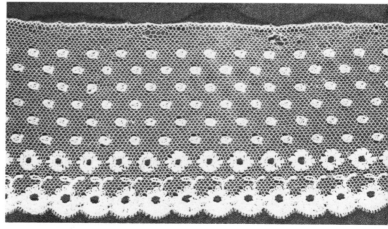

1790. Width 2½ins.

The designs became more wooden as the workers tried to speed up their output. Width 2½ins.

UNITED PROVINCES: THE NETHERLANDS

Holland is the northernmost, and was the richest of the United Provinces. The revolt of the Netherlands, from 1568-1609, won their independence. This poor and inconveniently organized group of provinces, during the seventeenth century, gradually became the richest country in Europe. The Dutch, ever sober and sensible, welcomed all comers and diversity of views. Unlike other countries at the time, they did not persecute anyone. Everyone lived peacefully. Private enterprise flourished and sea trade expanded. Amsterdam became the financial centre of Europe.

We do not know that lace was made in the Netherlands, but we do know that large quantities of a distinctive white lace, many with mirrored designs, were found there when lace collecting started in the last century. In the eighteenth century, the Dutch lost control of the seas and of sea commerce to the English. Their agriculture declined and a class of aristocrats called Regents developed. There was almost a civil war in 1787. In 1793, French revolutionary troops marched in and a republic was declared in 1795. Dutch lace followed the same designs and techniques until the middle of the eighteenth century. After that, those who could afford lace probably bought the most fashionable lace available.

In design, this lace seems to derive from the scalloped laces of the 1620s, where the mirrored design filled each scallop. The scallops lengthened in the 1630s and became a wavy edged straight shape in the 1640s. In the 1650s the edges became straight and meshed grounds made their appearance. The designs then copied the contemporary silks with sprigs and twisting tapes. However, the Dutch were conservative and their lace continued to have large headed flowers, like geometrical chrysanthemums, alternating with mirrored sprigs or cherubs, and was used well into the

These two almost identical pieces of lace show the uniformity of design in Dutch lace. The thread is fine and white, the workmanship is of the best. The lace is firm and hard-wearing, and the design pleasing. Both widths 1½ ins

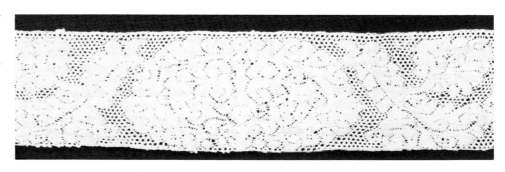

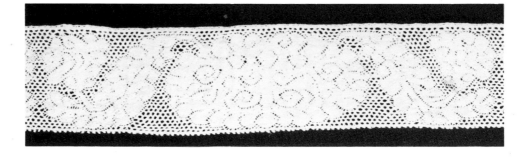

eighteenth century. It was made of a fine white thread and can be seen elegantly decorating both men's and women's collars in many portraits. Both sexes wore black, and the lace shows up beautifully. The restrained, hard-working Dutch continued to wear such plain but beautiful lace throughout their century of golden success. Unlike the Spanish, they never overdressed and displayed their wealth.

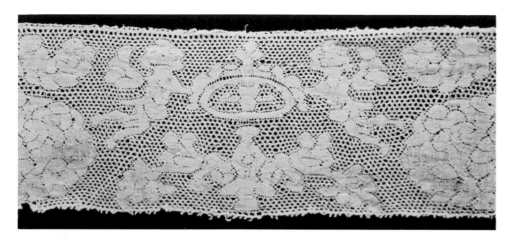

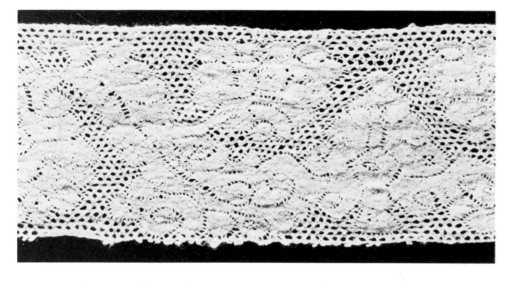

An amusing design, with wide mouthed cherubs. Width 2ins.

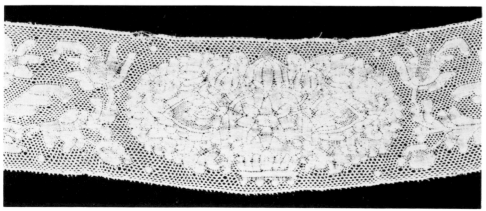

A close up showing the tightness of the work which makes it a hardwearing lace. Width 1½ins

This piece is made of particularly fine thread which shows clearly in the picture. The flower head is more elaborate than most. This is a superb example. Width 2¼ins.

POINT D'ANGLETERRE

Point d'Angleterre was made for a hundred years. It is a distinguished lace, beautifully designed and well made. Its name, which it bore in France throughout its existence, is a mystery; it was called point de Malines in England. Mrs. Palliser was certain that it was made at Brussels; really only a superior Brussels lace. Mrs. Jackson, another early writer on lace, was certain that it was made in England. Other writers think it was made in both countries. Point d'Angleterre is a fine lace and great quantities of it were made. It is a mixed lace and looks very like Brussels, but is always made of white thread, not the orangey colour of Brussels thread. The designers liked dark lines and thick 'black' rivulets are always found outlining the design. These dark lines, made by using tiny bars, are very noticeable. No point d'Angleterre was made in the nineteenth century.

Two details from an early lappet, 1690, showing the characteristics of point d'Angleterre — the superb quality of the work and the beauty of the design marked out by narrow 'black' outlines.

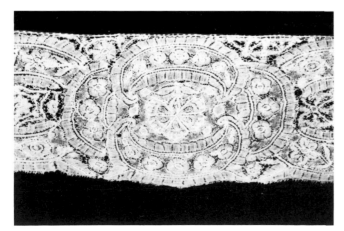 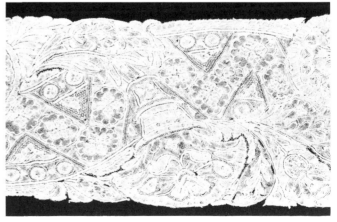

1690. This beautiful design is quite different from most contemporary lace. Width 2ins.

1700. This piece may have been a collar. The tiny bars making the 'black' rivulets are clearly to be seen. Width 4ins.

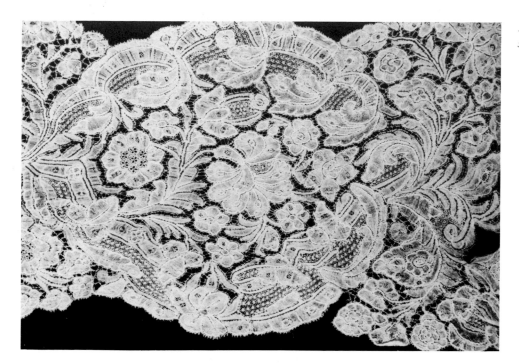

Detail. Beautifully made, one end is rounded, the other square. The fine stitches, white thread and delicate impractical edge make it look English.

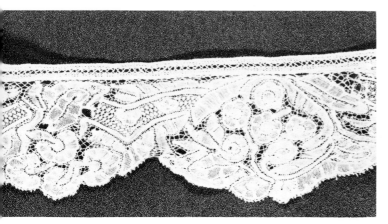

1710. The fond de neige strip balances the design. Width 2ins.

1720. This is a lovely flowing design with the cinq trous ribbon curling through it. There is a long repeat with different flowers.

18th century. This strip has a design of chalets, rock with flowing water, bird with leaf in its mouth, deer in flight, all separated by floral sprays. Length 34ins., width 3½ins.
The Metropolitan Museum of Art, gift by subscription, 1909. (09.68.216)

Bobbin lace, 1750. This strip shows the goddess Diana with her dogs. Length 29ins., width 3ins.
The Metropolitan Museum of Art, gift by subscription, 1909. (09.68.217).

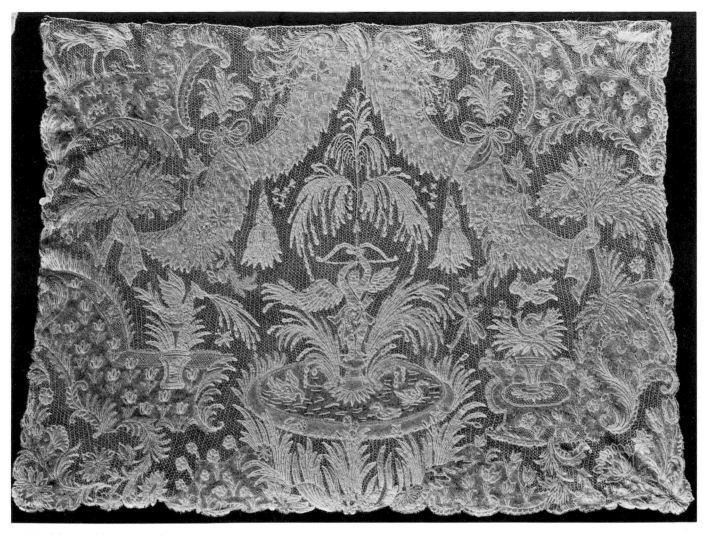

Mixed lace, 18th century. Cravat end.
The Metropolitan Museum of Art, gift of Mrs. Edward S. Harkness, 1948. (48.41.1)

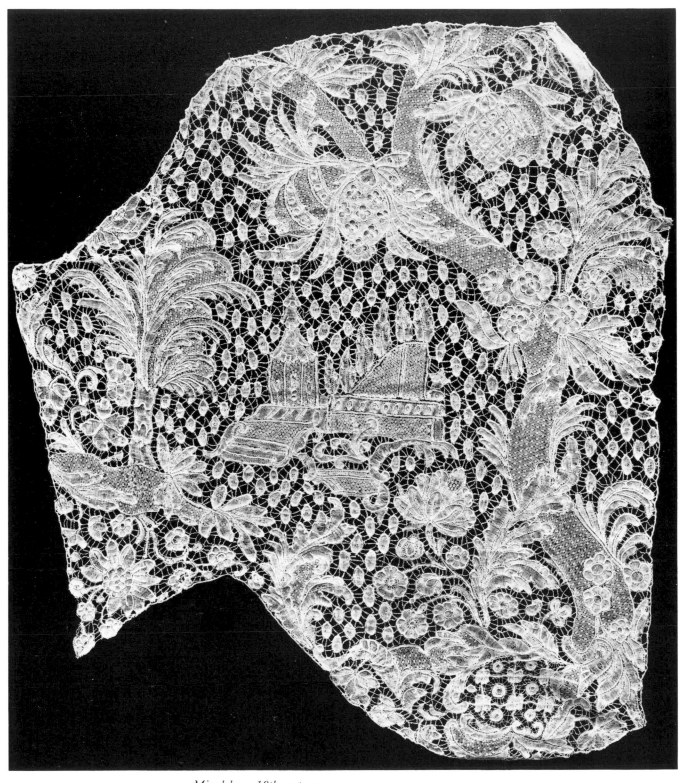

Mixed lace, 18th century.
The Metropolitan Museum of Art, bequest of Mrs. Jesse Seligmann, 1910. (10.102.31)

CHAPTER V

England

Lace was made in England throughout the seventeenth, eighteenth and nineteenth centuries. In the seventeenth century a great deal of needle lace was made. The design is a bit thin and the bars are elaborate giving the impression that it was made by amateurs. English ladies have always been marvellous needlewomen and needle lace is not difficult to make. There were merchants in London who prepared the white satin and designs for the making of raised or stumpwork and these shops may well have catered for lace makers as well. Shops of this kind are occasionally mentioned in diaries or letters of the period, but their existence is not explained. They were clearly a normal part of life. At this time too, and for another century, hollie point was worked at home, for baby clothes chiefly. Hollie point is an English stitch and does not appear to have been used on the Continent. It is a charming rectangular knotted stitch which was used for all sorts of semi-religious symbols. The back of the baby's bonnet illustrated on page 177 is typical.

Bobbin lace was made all over England. There are many references to laces in the Great Wardrobe Accounts, but these almost certainly referred to the laces used to tie together pieces of clothing. They were often ornamental and costly. The earliest sixteenth century references to real lace describe it as bone lace, so called because fish bones were used instead of pins which were too expensive for ordinary use.

At Blandford in Dorset wonderful lace was made until 1721, when a fire devastated the town and apparently wiped out the business. The leading manufacturers must have died and there was no one able to restore either morale or the town.

At Lyme, also in Dorset, fine lace was made throughout the seventeenth and eighteenth century. Some of this fine lace could have been point d'Angleterre. The lace shown on page 183 is unquestionably English. The poses of the portraits are Van Dyck poses taken from the famous sketches at Wilton. The English love of rounded shapes can be seen here too. The technique is superb and the thread fine. Flax was grown in East Devon, but of course there is no way of knowing whether or not English thread was used for this lace. The lace is very like Brussels lace, but is clearly not Flemish in origin.

It must be flatly stated here that English lace was made by English men and women. H.J. Yallop, Curator of the Allhallows Museum at Honiton has trudged the graveyards of the lace making areas, and all the graves of lace makers have English names. No known refugees ever settled in the west of England and there is no Dutch Reformed Church there. In places where refugees did settle, a church of their faith was one of the first buildings to be established. It must be remembered that lace makers were amongst the poorest people. They were not able to escape across the Channel after the riots following the repeal of the Edict of Nantes in 1685. Silver workers and cabinet makers came from a different level of society and could afford the journey.

From 1809 when it was invented by Heathcoat, English machine-made net led the world. By the 1840s some nets with woven designs were being made. Again England led the world and there was enormous interest in this novelty. Handmade lace however remained the ideal. It was called real lace, but was so expensive that only the rich could wear it.

English handmade lace of the nineteenth century was not as well designed nor as well made as its Continental rivals. The industry was not organized on a proper commercial basis. Lace was made in two main areas, but it was a declining industry that could not compete with machine-made lace, nor, at the top levels, with the Continental quality. The lace making areas were Devonshire and the East Midlands. Lace was sent from these places to London stores by local dealers. There does not seem to have been any control of standards from a fashion centre as there was in France. As the century passed, the lace makers were finally reduced to selling their

Needle lace, 1615. The roses and thistles identify this as English; so do the round shapes always used in England.
Victoria and Albert Museum.

1620. The Judgement of Solomon.
Victoria and Albert Museum

own work locally for what they could get for it. Obviously this was not much, and they gladly took whatever other work came their way. Various people like Mrs. Treadwin of Exeter tried to improve things, and ladies like Lady Trevelyan designed and ordered lace to her own designs. But these efforts were futile and handmade lace petered out.

Honiton lace from the nineteenth century can be recognized by the checkerboard fillings used in the centres of its very pretty flowers. Designs use lots of roses and simple flowers and there is no elaborate richness of design. Much of it is poor, in fact. A great deal of Honiton from the 1830s on was mounted onto machine net. From the middle of the century, Honiton made a lace called guipure, with bars instead of net joining the sprigs together. This new lace revived interest in Honiton and helped to encourage the best workers to make fine lace. All too many workers however, preferred to make easy slapdash lace that sold cheaply and in quantity. In the 1870s much seventeenth century Venetian lace as well as old Honiton was used again to make whatever was ordered. The lace sent down was called 'rags'. This expression tells its own tale.

Lace was made in the East Midlands during the eighteenth and nineteenth century. The manufacturers did not try to make quality lace. Like those of Le Puy, they aimed at a middle market. The prettiest of the laces was called Buck's Point and it was made during the first half of the century. A great deal of 'baby lace' was also made. This is a very narrow lace suitable for trimming babies' bonnets as well as underclothes, and household linen. All too soon the East Midlands workers found themselves competing with machine lace. Unfortunately the manufacturers did not try to compete in quality, but only in price. This was doomed to failure as the hand lace got cheaper and nastier and by the 1890s there were only a few hundred workers left.

Needle lace, 1630.
Victoria and Albert Museum.

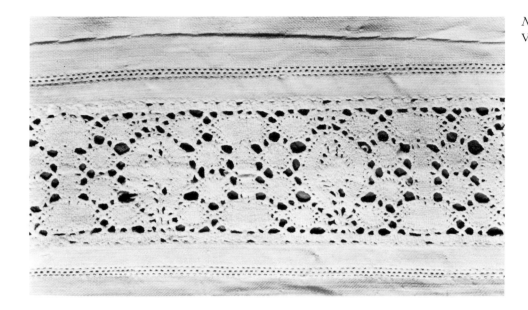

Needle lace, 1646.
Victoria and Albert Museum.

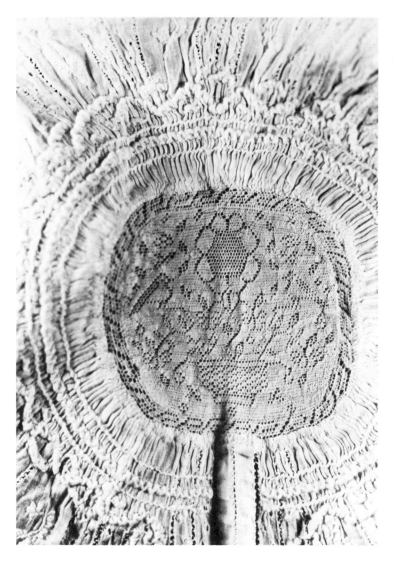

Needle lace, 1660. The back of a baby's bonnet, worked in hollie stitch. 2ins. across.

Lace made from hair, 1660.
Victoria and Albert Museum.

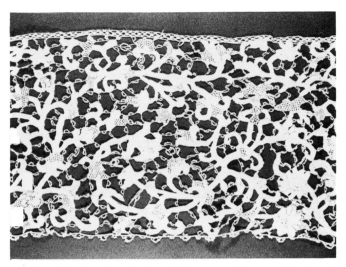

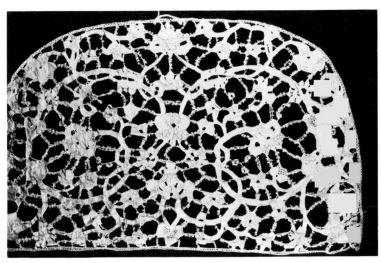

1630. *This piece is entirely needle lace, made in very fine thread and shows the S scrolls of an early piece. Width 6½ins.*

Cap back, 1640.

1650. *This lovely piece of lace has a long mirrored repeat. The spindly stems and realistic flowers are characteristically English. The stems are bobbin tapes and it is joined by needle lace; the flowers too are needle lace.*

Needle lace, 1700.
Victoria and Albert Museum.

Bobbin lace.
The Metropolitan Museum of Art, gift of Mrs. Anna Fairchild and of M.T.J., 1910. (10.92)

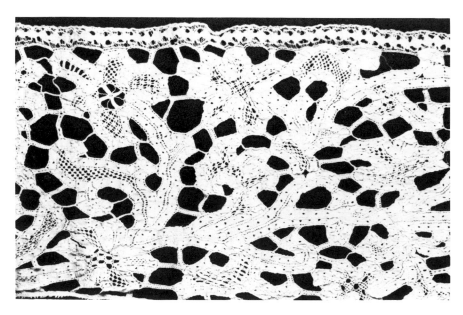

*1650. Bobbin tape joined by some
needle lace. Width 4½ ins.*

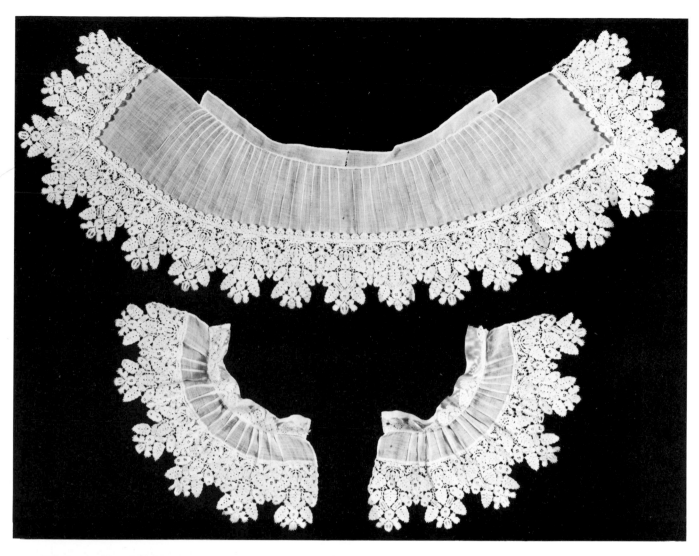

Bobbin lace, 1635. Set of collar and cuffs.
Victoria and Albert Museum.

Detail showing the leaves and plant shaped scallops in natural shapes which are so English in design.

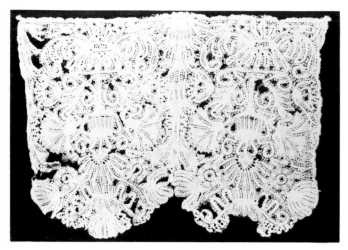 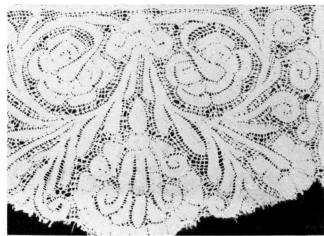

Above: 1630-40. This border of carnations illustrates the English love of flowers. 5ins. across.

Above right: This is a much more ordinary design, very close to Flemish ones of the same period, but these flowers are more natural with their curling petals. Width 3ins.

Lappet, 1700. The delicate, impractical edge, the fine bars, and the use of white thread show this to be English. Width 4ins.

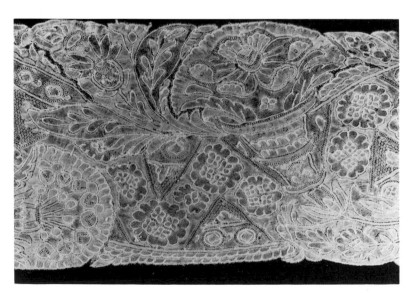

Collar, also English for the reasons explained above.

Bobbin lace, 1720-25. The portraits follow Van Dyck poses in paintings at Wilton House. The thread is white. Note the pretty, delicate but impractical edge to the lace. It was probably made at Blandford or Lyme, perhaps to celebrate the marriage of Sir Thomas Carew, 4th Bt., Sheriff of Devon to Dorothy West of Tiverton Castle in 1725. 'Marriage lace', ordered to mark a wedding, would have taken a year or two to make, but as the marriages took so long to arrange there was time.

Lappet ends. Width 3ins.

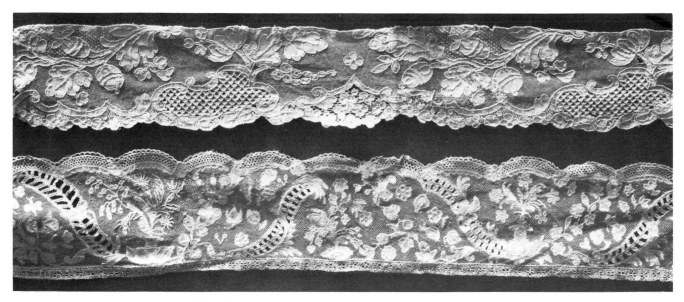

West Country bobbin lace, 1740.
The Metropolitan Museum of Art, gift of Mrs. Anna Fairchild and of M.T.J., 1910.
(10.92,10.93.6)

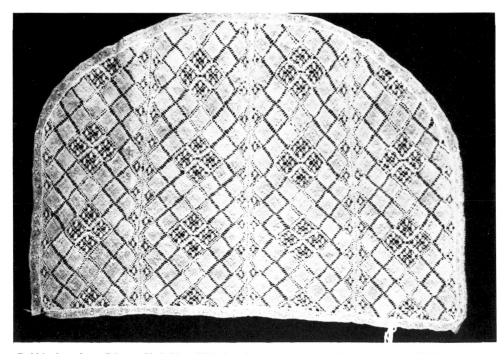

Bobbin lace from Ripon, Yorkshire. This lace has a neat geometric pattern. It is difficult to make as any mistake would show. Often it has a pretty, delicate, almost floral edging sewn to it. Mrs. Palliser, in her History of Lace, called it Ripon lace. It is not known whether she happened to buy her piece at Ripon, or if she knew it was made there. However, it is a specific type of English lace, wherever it was made.

This pair of lappets shows all the difficulties of English lace in the early eighteenth century. The English lace industry was never organized as was the French or Brussels manufacture. Lace was made at various places at different times in the West Country, Devon, Dorset, Somerset. Lace was sent weekly to London, not it seems to fill orders, but in the hopes that it would be sold. So much English lace of the first half of the eighteenth century has apparently mad designs, and yet is beautifully made of top quality thread, that one seeks an explanation. It may be that the Brussels business men thought they could use the English lace makers to fill their ever increasing orders. So fine thread and lace prickings were sent to the West Country, only in some cases to be made up into nonsensical lace. Even when, as in this case, the order was well carried out, the two ends were made differently. Remember that there would have been a year between the working of the two ends. Alternatively they may have been worked by two different people interpreting the design differently. The making of lace in Brussels was so strictly controlled that it could never have happened there. In addition, the thread is white, and so one must conclude that this pair of lappets is English.

Details showing the differences. The white thread, five petalled flowers, delicate edge and the oddly interpreted design all combine to make this recognisably English.

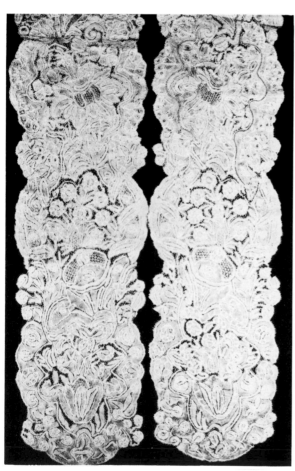

West Country lace, 1720. A pair of lappets that is not quite a pair. Width 4ins.

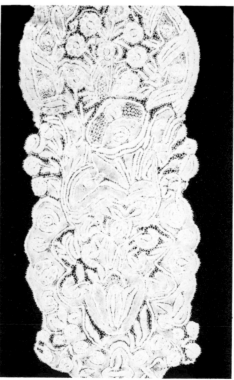

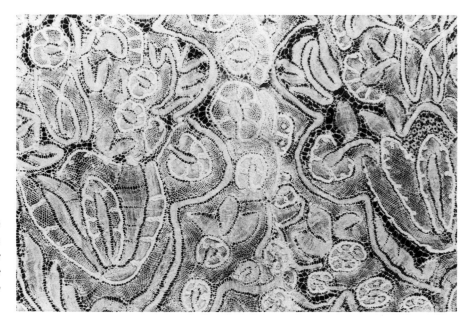

The two ends placed together so that the differences in interpretation can be seen. The edges overlap. The one on the right looks more like point d'Angleterre than ordinary English lace.

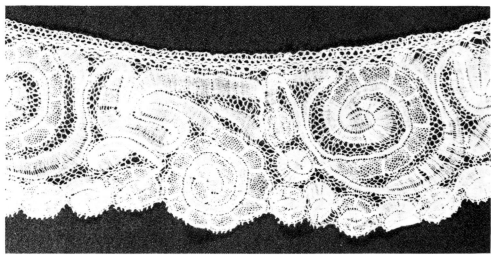

Right: The well known curious 'wormy' lace made in the West Country in the 1730s. Width 2ins.

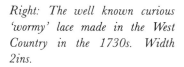

Below: One can only assume that the workers did not understand the prickings with which they were supplied. Widths 2ins. and 1½ins.

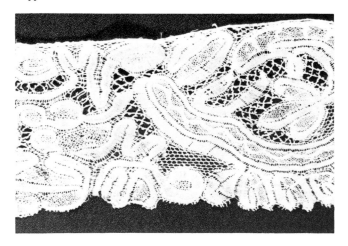

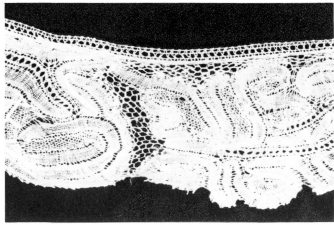

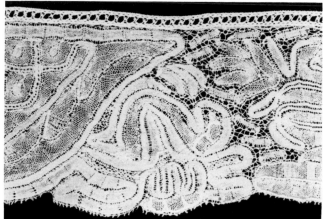

Above: Two views of the same oddly worked piece of lace. Width 2½ins.

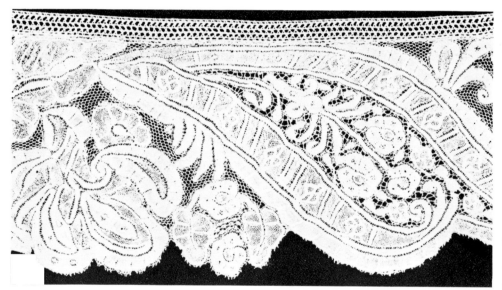

Left: Another strange interpretation of what may have been a good design. Width 4½ins.

Below: This worn cap back also with its five-petalled roses is edged with a piece of Mechlin with six-petalled roses.

Below left: This piece has five-petalled roses. Width 2½ins.

HONITON

Honiton is the best known name in English lace. Lace making must have started in the sixteenth century, since it was a flourishing industry by 1617. Devon was a well known weaving area in the sixteenth century and had a fulling mill in 1244. Flax was grown in East Devon. So all the necessary techniques were ready when the new textile, lace, appeared at the end of the sixteenth century. In the middle of the seventeenth century Fuller wrote that much lace is 'made in and about Honiton and weekly returned to London'. The ubiquitous Celia Fiennes wrote of Honiton which she visited in 1695, 'Here it is they make the fine bone lace in imitation of the Antwerp and Flanders lace'. If one looks at a lot of lace of 1690-1710 from Flanders or the West Country, one can distinguish two sorts. Brussels lace is orangey in colour. English lace is white. The Tudor rose, well known still in 1700, had five petals. Many of the white pieces have five petalled roses and many of the brownish pieces have six or seven petals. It cannot be proved that any of the lace certainly came from England or Brussels, but one can guess and hope to be right.

In the late eighteenth century, trolley lace, a lace with the pattern outlined with a thicker thread, came in and the Devon designs became very poor. When machine net was invented, particularly after Heathcoat's net of 1809, a great deal of applied lace was made at Honiton and very pretty it was. Later on the designs became slovenly and many efforts were made to improve them. Later again in the century, Honiton workers specialised in re-making old lace; ladies could send a bundle of old dirty lace to Honiton and receive in return a 'new' shawl or fichu.

Honiton, 1690. An early piece with a higgledy-piggledy design.
Victoria and Albert Museum.

Honiton. This design is much better organised.
Victoria and Albert Museum.

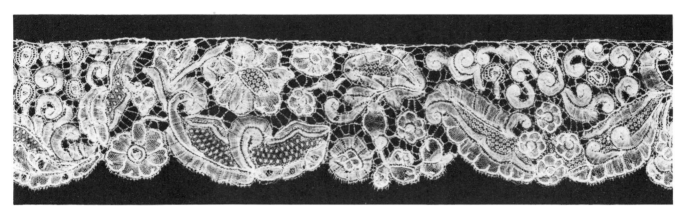

1700. The filling stitches are many and varied, and the design is well thought out.

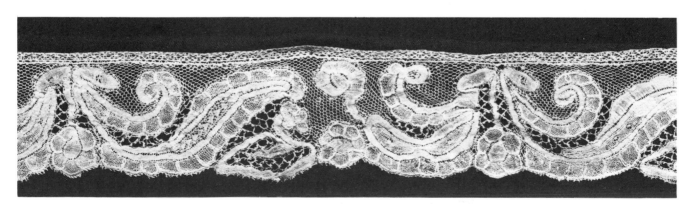

This design repeats neatly. There are fewer filling stitches and a ground is being attempted although the technique is still shaky.
Victoria and Albert Museum.

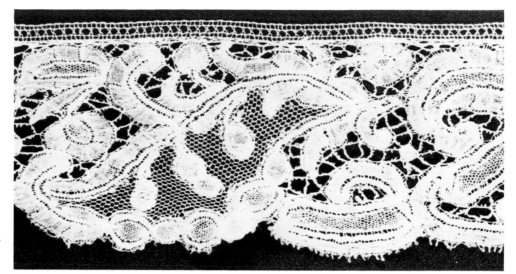

Honiton, 1710. A pretty piece of lace. Width 1¾ins.

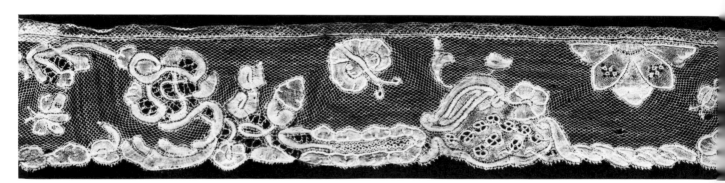

An attractive design of butterflies and flowers. The ground is still not under control.
Victoria and Albert Museum.

1730. The round roses in this design make it a typical piece of Honiton for this date.
Victoria and Albert Museum.

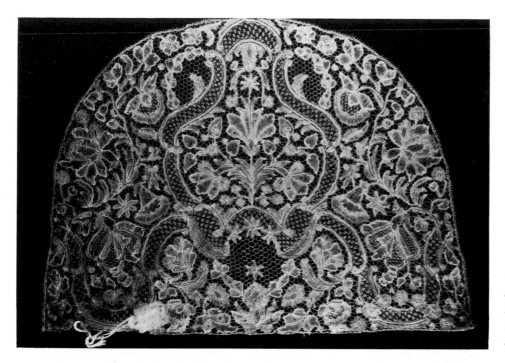

Cap back, 1750. The quality of design and workmanship made Honiton an important lace in the 18th century. It sold particularly well in France.

1780.
The Metropolitan Museum of Art, gift of Mrs. Anna Fairchild and of M.T.J., 1910. (10.93.6)

Midlands lace, 1775. Width 3½ins.

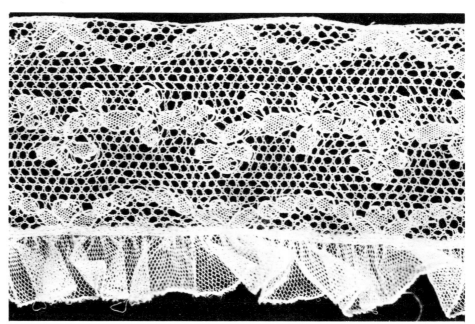

CHAPTER VI

Other Laces

In the sixteenth century, Spain was the richest and most powerful country in Europe. Huge supplies of gold came in each year with the treasure fleet. But Spain did not move with the times and the defeat of the Spanish Armada should have warned the king that his country had no solid base. Spain lived on its gold; no attempt was made to encourage the growth of a merchant class and no tolerance was shown towards any deviation in thought or action.

By contrast, the United Provinces were tolerant of any religious opinion and peacefully built up a merchant fleet that captured the world's markets. They also encouraged manufacturing. The seventeenth century, then, was the century of the Dutch.

Both countries bought in their lace, and so did any other country that could afford to; only the rich could afford the best Flemish, French or Italian lace. The less well off had to make do with whatever their own makers could provide. Local lace was usually an adaption of the nearest outstanding lace. Obviously it was easier in South Germany to copy Milanese lace, and for the Danes to copy Flemish lace. These laces are beautifully made in most cases and their charm lies in their slight differences from the standard designs. However, lace made in Central European countries is on the whole more interesting as folk art than as lace.

As the nineteenth century approached lace went out of fashion, and by the time it had returned to favour, lace manufacturers, led by Brussels, had learned to make lace cheaply. Thus there was plenty of lace available at all prices, and it was made very widely in Europe. This chapter deals mainly with laces made earlier, in the eighteenth century. The debt to Milan is apparent in South German lace; Hungarian lace, made further away, is more distinct.

Hungary, 18th century. Note the birds. Width 5ins.

Southern Germany, 18th century. The debt to Milan is clear. Width 7ins.

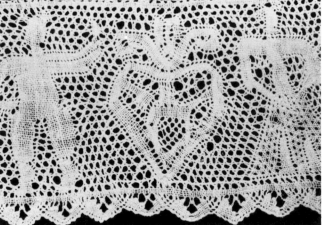

Above: These rather coarse laces come from further north in Germany. The designs are charming. Widths 3ins. and 4ins.

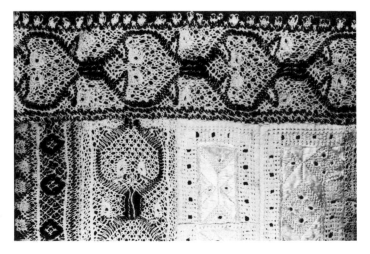

Middle East, 19th century. A black and white lace. Width 12ins.

SPAIN

A great deal of money was spent on dress in Spain. Gold and silver braids and multicoloured ribbons were much used in all parts. When lace became available, an enormous amount of it was sold to Spain from Venice and other Italian cities. It was used by the Church as well as for dress. Some lace must have been made in places like Barcelona and Seville as there are references to this in documents, but the huge sums sent to Italy, Flanders and France make it clear that most of the lace used in Spain was imported. When the convents were suppressed in 1835, the amount of lace that appeared on the market was incredible. The so-called point d'Espagne, Venetian lace made for the Spanish market, remains cheaper than contemporary Venetian pieces, even today. Point d'Espagne can be distinguished from its Venetian counterpart by the long 'worms' that form the topmost layer of the design. It appears, however, to have been made in Venice. The bobbin lace made in Spanish Flanders was very fine. The ground had a tiny rectangle where the threads met.

The only original contribution to lace making from Spain comes in the form of the 'rueda'. These are circles, made by stretching threads back and forth across a circular frame to meet in the centre. The circle is then woven with a design with a needle and thread. This may have started as a wheel made to fill drawn fabric work but the makers soon developed a special technique using circular frames. These ruedas are much loved in South America where the centre point is thought of as the radiant sun. It is thus linked to the ancient Amerindian religions. Each country in South America has its own favourite designs. It is sad that no designer of genius has ever been able to make a new and exciting textile from these circles.

Point d'Espagne, 1670. This was a Venetian lace made for the Spanish market. Width 3ins.

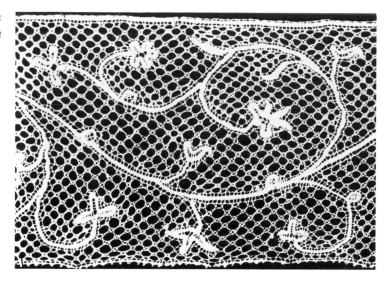

Spain, 1710. Bobbin lace. This illustrates the unusual Spanish ground.
Victoria and Albert Museum.

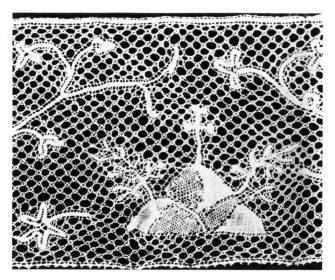

Spanish bobbin lace, 1710. A section from a long piece of Spanish church lace.
Victoria and Albert Museum.

Another view.

Ruedas from Bolivia.
Victoria and Albert Museum.

*Rueda, said to have come from the
Philippines. 5½ ins. across.*

RUSSIA

The lace shown here was made in the nineteenth century. The wearing of lace had become a political matter. The Russian royal family encouraged Russian arts and crafts for patriotic reasons. The Princesses were often photographed wearing lace ruffles on their clothes, and those who supported them followed their example. The use of coloured threads, and the rounded shapes makes this lace distinctive.

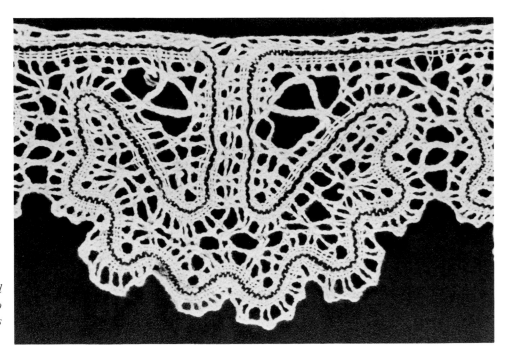

Russia. The simple technique used in the making of this lace points to its peasant origin. Blue thread is used in this piece. Width 3¾ ins.

White lace. Width 2¼ ins.

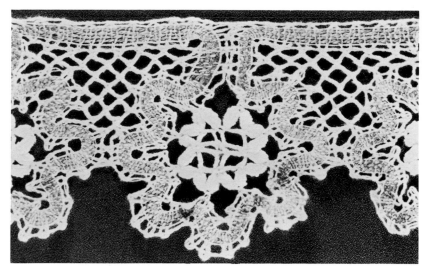

Blue, brown and white threads make this a distinctive lace. Width 2¼ ins.

Below: A very different pattern, but again the same colours.

Below left: The same colours are used in this piece too.

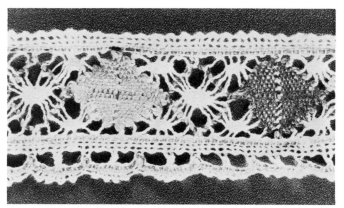

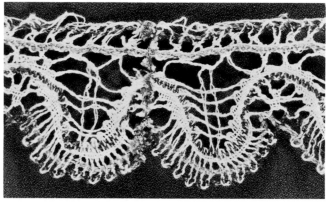

India, 19th century. A great deal of needle lace was made in India at this time. It is easily identified as the flowers do not look European, and the borders are not in the traditional designs. The thread is white.

U.S.A.

There are half a dozen pieces of black lace at the Historical Society in Ipswich, Massachusetts, U.S.A. These are said to have been made there commercially in the 1790s. At that time the lace manufacturers of Flanders were searching for markets to replace the French market lost after the French Revolution. With no documentation one cannot be sure, therefore, that this lace was made in America. It is to be hoped that the Society will encourage work to be done on this interesting subject.

In the seventeenth century, many thousands of English women made lace. No doubt many lace makers went to America and must have made lace there. Such lace is known, but there is no record of any commercial lace making. However, one must remember that the making of porcelain in America was only discovered quite recently; there is a lot more research to be done.

CHAPTER VII

The Nineteenth Century

During the nineteenth century the making of lace by hand was virtually destroyed by the development of cheaper machine-made lace. The century opened with the trade in depression. The lightness of lace was unsuited to the classical designs then in fashion and the concept of lace for the rich only went against all the current revolutionary ideas. The production of handmade lace had almost disappeared by the end of the century. However, the first machine-made nets had come into commercial use in 1763. By 1800, there was plenty of it. It was made on a stocking frame and like knitting it easily unravelled. In 1809, Heathcoat patented his net machine and this machine which made a recognisable net, not far removed from the handmade grounds, revolutionised the industry. For the next twenty years many people worked hard to improve the machines and by 1850 patterned lace had appeared. In the meantime, the net made by the Heathcoat machine and its successors worked wonderfully well as a base for embroidery. Every sort of darning stitch and chain stitch were used. The lace manufacturers of Brussels intelligently made applied lace. The motifs were made by needle or bobbin or both and applied to the net. This net has a slightly crisp feel, quite different from the needle or bobbin grounds. This feel makes dating easier. From 1810-30, a great deal of this embroidered net was made, as well as bobbin and needle lace for the richer clients. Lace was at last becoming available for the ordinary woman.

All through the century, old lace of the finest quality was much prized for full dress. In *Vanity Fair*, Thackeray describes how Becky Sharp stole the family 'point lace' and wore it with a fine piece of brocade, also stolen, to court. This took place about 1820. Lace was out of fashion, but had to be worn at court. Throughout the centuries court dress has always required old-fashioned clothes. Trains and feathers in the 1930s are an example that many can still remember.

Throughout these decades there was much use of embroidered muslin with or without lace, on bed draperies and curtains. During the century lace came to be used more and more on household linens. Hundreds of thousands of yards of lace must have been used on sheets and pillowcases and table linen and anti-macassers.

1800-1830

Until about 1815 the straight edged lace of the end of the eighteenth century continued to be made. This narrow lace, of about one and a half to two inches, was used at the neck and around the hem of the narrow, straight and elegant dresses. Blonde was much admired for shawls or stoles. Blonde is a lace which, having originally been made of silk, was so called because of its natural silk colour. It was also made in black. Blonde was made in a great many different places from Spain to the East Midlands in England

Brussels, 1800-1810. Coverlet; Diana and Endymion. Bobbin lace with needle lace details. Length 88ins., width 82ins.

The Metropolitan Museum of Art, gift of Mrs. Edward S. Harkness. 1944 (44.91.1)

and all over France and Belgium. It was a very pretty lace with a light ground and heavy leaves or flowers to give it weight.

The manufacturers at Alençon, particularly the five leading companies, kept going by making and selling embroidery. A great deal of white work was used at that time, not only for dress but also for bed hangings and curtains. By keeping a nucleus of lace makers going, the Alençon manufacturers were ready to increase production when lace finally started to come back into fashion. The Brussels manufacturers too were ready to make lace when fashion turned that way. The Alençon firms opened offices in Paris, as did manufacturers of other laces like Le Puy and Chantilly. Paris was the fashion centre of the world and so the lace makers were in a position to cope with each whim of fashion.

Scallops returned in about 1815 and remained in fashion throughout the

Alençon, 1815. A handkerchief embroidered with lace stitches. The manufacturers kept going with work like this.

Detail.

1820s. Shawls became an important accessory. Every lady needed several, light for summer, heavy for winter, and when it was really cold, a mantle. This last was a shawl which became more and more shaped until it became a jacket. Once crinolines came in, women could wear layers and layers of wool on their legs, hidden by the full skirt, so only a short garment was needed for warmth. The pretty scalloped laces of the 1820s and '30s had enchanting flowers, natural looking and light. Black lace also reappeared at this time. It was very delicate and pretty. Both black and white laces had a great deal of ground and the flowers were delicately outlined, not solid at all. The scallops were usually edged with flower heads or petals. Brussels applied lace was particularly suited to these airy designs. Needle or bobbin lace was also made on its own grounds, or needle lace with a bobbin ground, as well as the cheaper lace applied to machine net.

Lille, 1800. Bobbin lace. Width 1¾ ins.

Lille. A monotonous design.

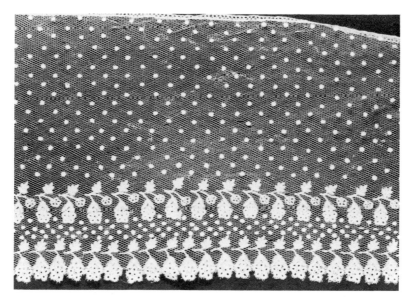

Brussels, 1810. Needle lace applied to bobbin ground. Width 4½ins.

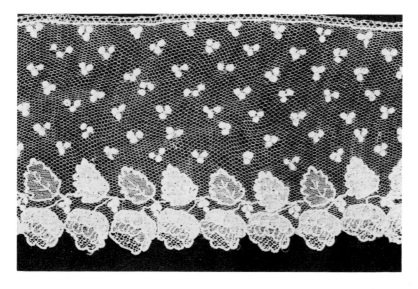

Alençon. A fine piece of handmade needle lace. Width 3ins.

Alençon. Handmade lace.

Brussels, 1820. Applied lace, needle lace on machine net — a lovely lace. Width 4½ins.

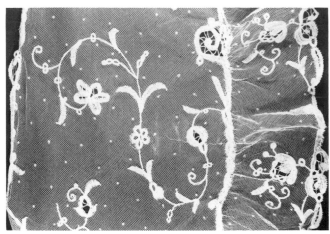

Honiton, 1820. The bobbin lace motifs have been applied to machine net.

Brussels. Needle lace applied to a bobbin ground. Width 4ins.

Brussels. A double collar of applied lace on machine net.

Mechlin. A very fine piece of handmade lace. 2¾ins.

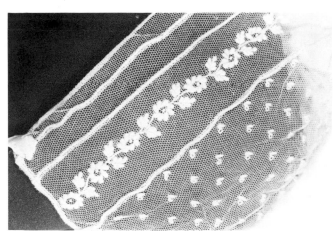

Brussels. Applied lace on a baby's bonnet.

Chantilly, 1830. A hat veil. The thread has been run into a machine net.

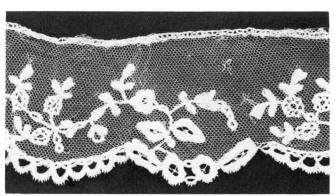

Lille, 1830. Handmade bobbin lace. Width 3½ins.

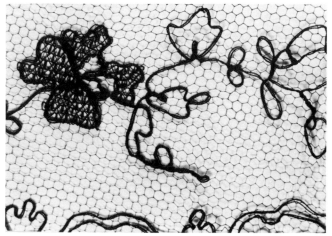

Detail.

Brussels. Mixed lace applied to machine net. Width 4ins.

Brussels. Needle lace on a needle ground. Width 1½ins.

Chantilly. The lace is handmade. Width 16½ins.

1830-1840

During the 1830s, the scallops on lace became shallower and the designs covered more of the area. The designs no longer lay separated by areas of mesh, but gradually took over the lace.

At this time, Queen Adelaide, wife of William IV, went to Malta. There she not only built a church but also started the making of Maltese lace. This she organized by bringing in teachers from Genoa. Maltese lace brought a great deal of money into the islands all through the century. Even today, one can see lace being made on Gozo.

All over Europe there were social stirrings. The growth of the middle classes associated with the industrial revolution led by the English created a whole new market for lace. Cheaper laces were made to suit all levels of this market, but during this decade, pretty bordered laces were the most in demand.

In the late 1830s as skirts became larger and fuller, they were balanced by berthas. These were collars of wide lace gathered onto an open neckline. They could be matched with a flounce on the bottom of the skirt or with a gathered cuff as on Queen Victoria's wedding dress. At this time too, Valenciennes came back into fashion as a lace for home use, for peignoirs and underclothes, for little girls' dresses and on handkerchiefs. Throughout the century, handkerchiefs were important. At times the central pieces of cloth were so small that their uselessness was apparent, but as in the seventeenth century they were an expensive accessory.

England. Blonde lace, worn at the coronation of Queen Victoria, 1837, by the wife of the Postmaster General. Note the rose, leek and thistle.

Below: Alençon, 1835. A needle made lace. Width 3½ ins.

Below right: England. Bucks point. In poor condition, but a fine handmade bobbin lace with a kat ground.

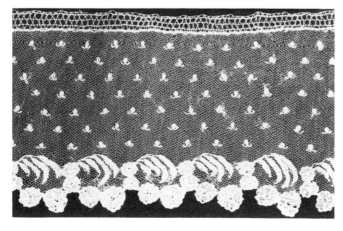

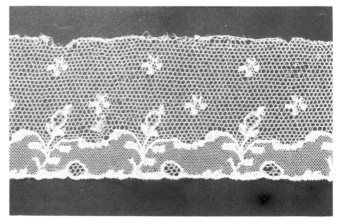

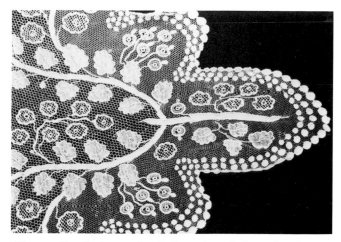

Alençon. Details from a shawl. From the technique, thread and design, it must have been made in about 1840. This piece of lace is of superb quality and must have cost an enormous amount. It was appreciation of this kind of quality work that kept Alençon lace going throughout the 19th century.

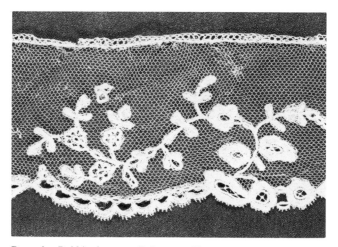

Lille. A pretty cuff made of machine net with hand embroidery. The edging is handmade. Width 3½ins.

Brussels. Bobbin lace applied to machine net; some needle work. Width 2½ins.

Mechlin. Handmade lace of poor quality. Width 3¾ins.

1840-1850

This decade, known as the hungry forties because of the Irish famine, was also a decade of social unrest and revolutionary ideas.

Lace design developed as various new techiques were invented. True machine lace did not appear until about 1850, but there were many attempts to make it, aided by much handwork. The designers were trying to copy handmade lace and so the designs developed slowly and predictably.

Lille, 1840. A coarse furnishing lace. The ground is clearly seen. Width 5ins.

Lille, 1840. A fine, delicate piece which would ruffle prettily. Width 4ins.

Lille. Handmade on its own ground. Width 3ins.

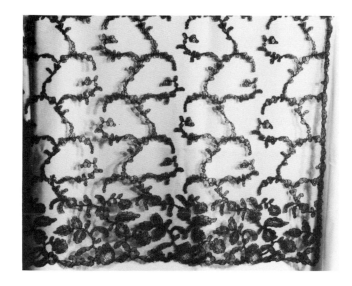

Above: Chantilly, 1840. A handmade parasol cover with the extra piece that lay on top.

Above left: Bobbin lace applied to machine net. Width 19½ins.

The end section of a handmade mantilla.

Chantilly, 1840-50. Machine net with much hand work. Width 6ins.

Width 2½ins.

Mechlin, 1845. Part machine-made, the thick threads have been put in by hand. Width 2¾ins.

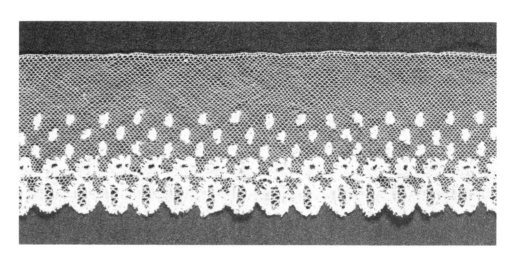

Mechlin. Made in the same way. Width 2¼ins.

Alençon. This piece which is entirely handmade is said to have belonged to the Empress Eugenie. Width 7½ins.

By 1850 caps were worn all day and in the evening by women of all classes. The lappets, which usually hung clear, were round ended and were at times made in with a wholly lace cap. At other times, caps were made of muslin with lace ruffles and ribbons. Even bonnets had lace trimmings as well as ribbons and flowers. Dresses were made with big sleeves and under them were placed lace sleeves with cuffs. Many of these can be seen at sales, and thousands must have been made. Patterned lace made by machine now appeared. Machine lace copied Mechlin, Valenciennes, Chantilly and Buckinghamshire laces. The manufacturers used the same designers and the lace was very fine indeed. A lot of handwork was used on the machine lace. Thick threads were run in on the Chantilly, for instance, and with some of them it is very hard to tell which are machine-made and which handmade.

In the 1850s and '60s, lace gradually became heavier in design as Maltese lace became fashionable. This geometric lace was copied all over Europe and was usually made of silk. It came in white or black. Maltese lace

ushered in an era of heavy rich looking lace. The Brussels manufacturers started making Duchesse lace, although their beautiful point de gaze remained the best of all laces. Point de gaze is so beautiful that it always sold well in spite of what must have been its enormous cost. It was the only completely new lace to be made in the nineteenth century. Its elaborate workmanship and enchanting rich design made it an unforgettable sight. There is no other lace like it. With it too, came the technique of shading. This makes the flowers very natural looking indeed.

Lace was much appreciated at this time, and it became for the rich a sign of wealth. A new class of lace wearers now emerged. These were the women who, thanks to all the new manufacturing, could afford lace for the first time. They wanted pretty, not too expensive lace, and they got it. Machine-made lace was much cheaper than handmade, but it was so well made and well designed that no one can have minded wearing it. The manufacturers also discovered how to make lace wide enough to be used in dressmaking. Very wide borders were woven to set off the fabric and make a well balanced dress.

Lille. Border with design of crowned eagles alternating with monogram and bees below laurel wreath. The monogram is of Napoleon III, Louis Napoleon. The Metropolitan Museum of Art, gift of Mrs. Albert Blum, 1953. (53.162.44)

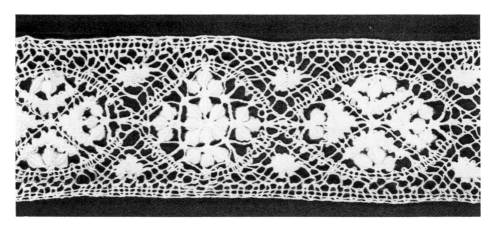

The true Maltese lace is at the top. Beautifully made of fine silk, the square leaves identify it as truly Maltese. The piece below is English. It is also well made; the leaves are slim and elegantly shaped.

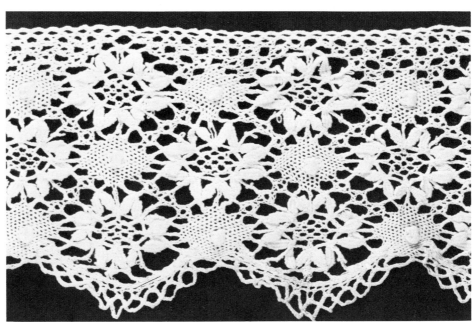

Width 3ins.

Chantilly, 1850-60. Handmade fichu, a decorative accessory.

France. A fine piece of machine lace with the thick threads run in by hand. The design and the lace are light.

214

Two handmade Chantilly borders, made to be worn together. Entire trousseaux would be ordered with yards of lace in matching design but in different widths.

Width 12ins.

Width 4½ins.

Chantilly, 1850-60. Much hand work has been added to the machine net. Width 6ins.

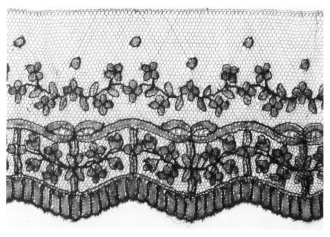

Again all the outlines have been put in by hand. Width 4¼ins.

Width 7½ins.

Mechlin, 1850-60. Two hand-made pieces. Widths 5ins. and 6½ins.

Width 7½ins.

Width 6ins.

Point de gaze, 1860. This beautiful lace was launched in Brussels in 1852. It combines bobbin and needle lace and its ground is the old delicate looped buttonhole stitch. It is very filmy and light. This lace must have been very expensive to make. It sold extremely well in spite of its price as it was so beautifully made and the designs were lovely. Note the extra petals added to the roses. This elaborate lace could not have been designed at any other period, does not copy any other lace, and is the finest lace made at that time.

Brussels, second half of 19th century. Needle lace border in point de gaze. Length 2yds. 31ins., width 7½ins.

The Metropolitan Museum of Art, bequest of Catherine D. Wentworth, 1948. (48.187.594)

Brussels, 19th century. Parasol cover, needle lace on machine ground, with chinoiserie motifs.
The Metropolitan Museum of Art, gift of Mrs. Heyward Cutting, 1942. (42.150.26)

1860-1870

In the 1860s, lace became more and more rich and opulent. The flowers were looped in ribbons and surrounded by ornate sculptural patterns. The designs are very handsome and could not have been made at any other date. They were echoed in the elaborate wallpapers and furnishings of the period. In contrast to all this opulence, Le Puy brought out a geometric lace called Cluny. It is rigidly neat and tidy and follows the fashion for Maltese of ten years before. By the end of the 1860s, blonde was only being used as trimmings, and most of it was machine-made. In its place came 'Spanish' lace. This was a heavy edged machine-made lace. The edge was trimmed with leaves or flowers, and it is not unlike the blonde of the 1840s.

Brussels, 19th century. Needle lace border, point de gaze.
The Metropolitan Museum of Art, gift of Mrs. Heyward Cutting, 1942. (42.50.24)

Point de gaze. Cut to 8ins.
Private Collection.

France, 1860. The heavy edged so-called Spanish lace, machine-made. Width 4ins.

This lace of extraordinary design was originally made with its own ground, probably chantilly or kat stitch. It has been remounted on to a piece of fine machine net. The whole repeat is shown. This piece of lace was shown at the big exhibition of lace at The Metropolitan Museum of Art in New York in 1922.

Above: Brussels, 1860. Point de gaze, mixed lace. Width 2¼ins.

Above left: Duchesse, all hand-made. Width 1½ins.

1860. Duchesse. This section of a very large piece of lace shows the quality of the work. Width 11ins.

1870-1880

1870 was a bad year for lace. Eugenie, the French Empress, loved it and wore a great deal, but when the Second Empire fell, the whole attitude to lace changed. Machine-made lace was winning the battle. Chantilly, defeated, stopped making handmade lace. Chantilly had been, for decades, the best loved of all laces, and its closure was a sad loss to the lace world.

However, it did become fashionable to make lace at home as interest in homemade things generally grew. Everything needed was sold together in a kit — pattern, threads and needles. This lace was made by darning net

A kit which could be bought for lace making in the 1870s.

The results were not worth the trouble!

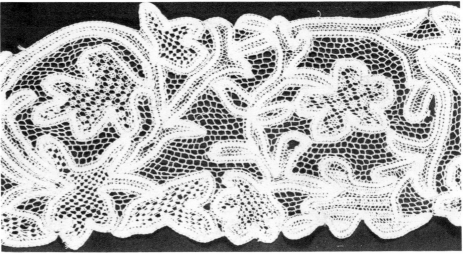

or by putting tapes together with needle lace stitches. It is not attractive!

During the 1870s, lace making in the Midlands ceased. The machine-made copies of Valenciennes became so like the handmade ones that it is virtually impossible to tell them apart. Very light soft lace was the fashion. People wore soft fichus, and light airy designs. There was a growing interest in old lace. With the founding of the School at Burano, Venetian lace of the seventeenth century became fashionable and so did the colour ecru. How much lace has been damaged by being dipped into tea or coffee, we cannot tell, but from that day to this, it has been done. Tea can be washed out, but coffee cannot.

Gradually fashion swung to heavier laces. Flowers seem to have been forgotten and prettiness was not wanted. It was a formal world and fashionable smartness was more desirable than becoming prettiness. Colours were loud and shapes were clumsy. Everything in the house had a cover. Many mats were used on tables and pianos, but they were often trimmed with braid rather than with lace. Lace was of course used when things needed to be washed, on table linen and underclothes, and as an accessory such as the Valenciennes handmade scarf.

England, Honiton, 1870. End of a fichu. Applied lace was made at Honiton for decades. There was much variation in the quality of design.

Brussels, 1870. A fine mixed lace. Width 1in.

Brussels, 1870. Duchesse, made of very fine thread.

IRELAND

During the seventeenth and eighteenth centuries, lace was made at home. Here and there, gifted amateurs taught classes. There was no organised lace making until Mrs. John Grey Porter returned from her honeymoon in Italy in 1816 with the idea of applying cambric to machine net and adding lace stitches. Mrs. Porter organised a school at Carrickmacross, aided by various neighbours and excellent teachers. This lace was still being made in this century.

Limerick lace was organised commercially by an Englishman. The designs were worked in stitches with hook or needle on to machine net. Limerick lace too lasted into this century.

Above: Ireland, Carrickmacross, 1850. This very pretty applied lace was always well worked to good designs.

Above left: Ireland, 1860. A collar, made as carefully as the older one above.

Left: Ireland, Carrickmacross. A beautiful wedding veil.
Private Collection.

Above: Ireland, Limerick, 1850. Embroidered net, which was made from 1829 to the end of the century. Width 7ins.

Ireland, Youghal. Needle lace, with foliated scroll designs, in centre of each a star flower. Width of bottom piece 4¾ ins.

The Metropolitan Museum of Art, gift by subscription, 1909. (09.68.516)

Needle lace was also made in Ireland. Youghal is the best known.

Ireland, Youghal. Needle lace. Width 4ins.
The Metropolitan Museum of Art, gift of Mrs. Julian James, 1911. (11.44)

Ireland, Youghal. Needle lace.
The Metropolitan Museum of Art, purchased by subscription, 1909. (09.68.515)

Irish crochet is world famous. It was easy to work in the home and needed no elaborate equipment. When it is good it is very very good and when it is bad it is horrid!

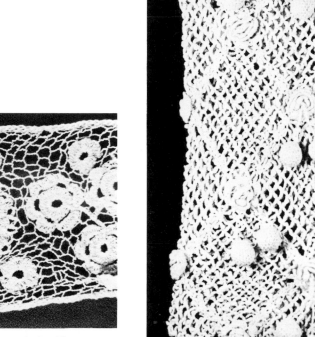

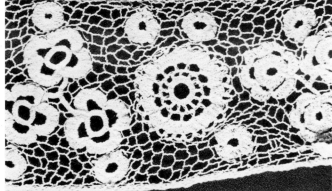

Ireland. Crochet: the design and execution are deplorable.

Ireland. A crochet bag, beautifully made, it is a charming accessory.

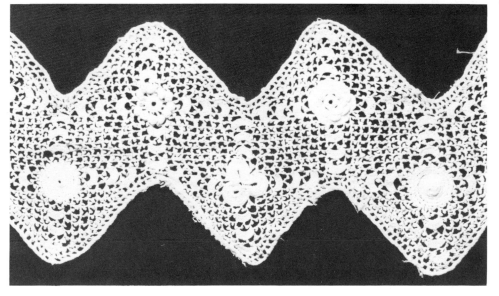

Ireland, 1860. This heavy looking crochet lace is soft and pretty. It does not compare in quality with any of the more sophisticated laces. Width 1½ins. to 2ins.

Ireland. A most beautifully made collar. The crochet base has needle lace additions. It is a sophisticated and interesting design which would have looked fashionable anywhere in the civilised world.

Ireland, 1880-90. Collar. A beautiful design, it is like no other lace — crochet with needle work added.

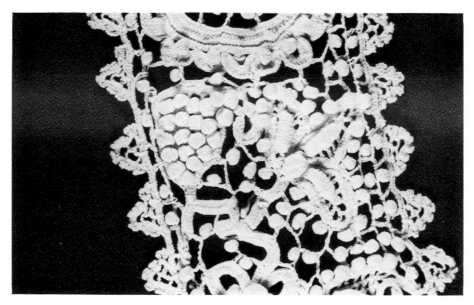

Detail.

BURANO

Burano is a small island in the Venetian lagoon. It is a charming place and still has a lace school. Lace has probably been made there for centuries. The needle lace shown in the Museum looks like ordinary Venetian lace except that the thread is not top quality. Of the older laces, the best known ones are those of the 1770s and 1780s. They look rather like Alençon except for the ground. This is worked the length of the piece, not across it, which gives it a distinctive ladder-like look. The lace makers of Burano could not afford linen thread; it is therefore mixed with cotton. This gives the lace a rough woolly look as the cotton becomes fuzzy. In the early nineteenth century it was discovered how to make the threads smooth. This was done by heating it in 'gas'. After that, much lace was made of cotton or of mixed thread. It feels less hard, but otherwise is the same. Lace making at Burano died out around 1800 as it did in so many places.

In 1872 however, there was a dreadful winter, the lagoon froze and the people of Burano faced starvation. Several Italian ladies arranged for an old lace maker to teach several young ones, and they in turn taught in the School set up opposite the Church. It is still there, but as always with lace manufacturing, it has had its ups and downs. To begin with, marvellous copies of old lace were made with the finest threads. Then all too soon, the quality of the thread went down and a great deal of rather poor copies were made. In the 1920-30 period place-mats, table mats and so on, were made as copies of Alençon. They sold well and many thousands were made. This 'Alençon' can be distinguished from real Alençon by the colour of the thread. Burano lace always seems to be the same ugly dark ecru colour. One soon learns to recognize it.

Burano, 18th century. A copy of Alençon, but on a Burano ground which was worked lengthwise and has a curious stepladder look.

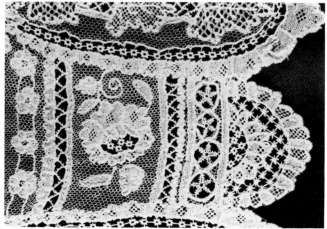

Burano, 1875. This piece is made of the best thread, available after a charity had been set up in 1872. The colour is ecru, the design uninspired.

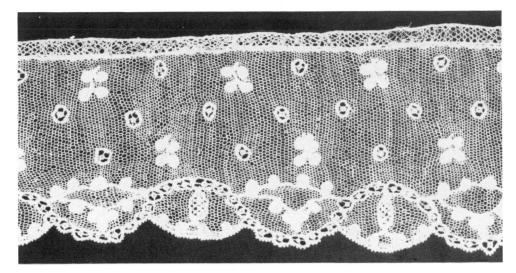

Burano, 1780. The fuzzy cotton thread can be easily seen. Width 2¼ ins.

An example of the wonderful workmanship of the 1880s. Width 8½ ins.

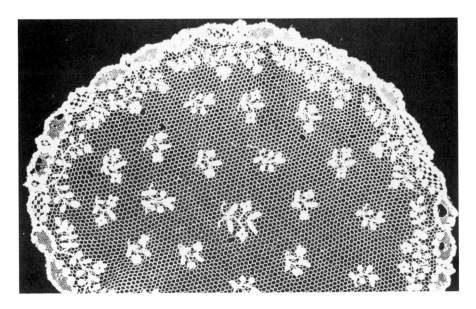

A place mat copying Alençon. They were much used in the 1920s.

Chantilly, 1870. Stole. Machine-made. Width 20ins.   *Handmade in very soft black silk.*

A machine piece. Cut to 6ins.

Honiton lace applied to kat ground. Cut to 12ins.   *Detail showing ground.*

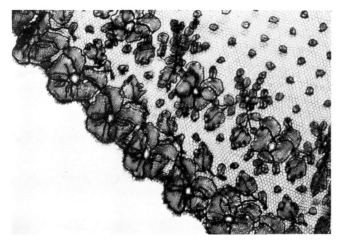

Chantilly. Hat veil, machine-made with hand work.

Chantilly. A great deal of hand work is obvious. Width 2½ins.

Chantilly. Collar. This lace is applied to a Pusher machine-made net.

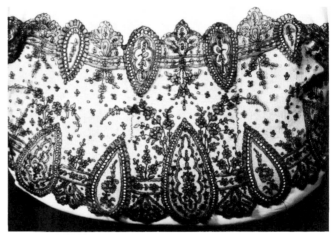

Fichu. Handmade. Width 12½ins.

Detail.

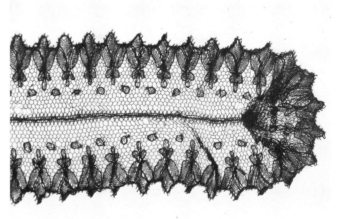

A run of the mill piece with Pusher machine-made ground. Width 3½ins.

Chantilly. A large handmade shawl. The leaves are 8ins. in length.

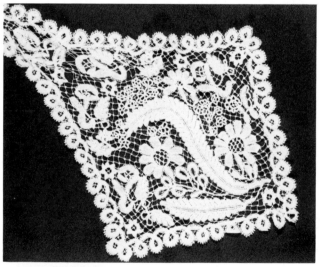

Chantilly, 1850-60. An enormous handmade shawl. This detail shows where the joining stitch would have been.

Honiton. A stocking front.

Chantilly, 1850-60. A soft lace made on the Levers machine. Width 9ins.

Chantilly. Width 3½ins.

Chantilly, 1870. Lappet.

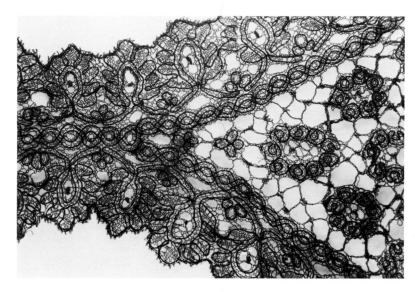

Detail.

Valenciennes. Machine-made, a striking piece. Width 14ins.

Valenciennes. Handmade, with threads added to make the design stand out, as has been done to the piece on the left. Width 4ins.

Blonde, 1875. Machine-made and very fragile; silvery grey in colour.

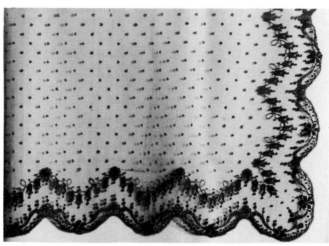

Chantilly, 1875. Stole. Handmade. Width 35ins.

Detail of machine-made Chantilly.

Chantilly, 1875. Machine-made. Width 13ins.

Chantilly. Machine-made. By this time any black lace was called Chantilly and it was made all over Northern France. Width 5ins.

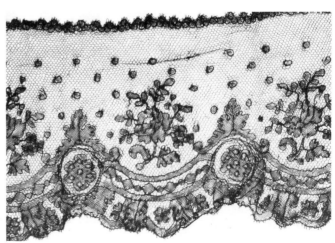

Machine-made. As can be seen, a light delicate lace. Width 4½ins.

Three laces of 1875.

Germany. Width 2ins.

Germany. A typical piece of German lace of this period. The ground is Spanish. Width 2¾ins.

England. Torchon lace made in the East Midlands. These were laces made for the middle market. Width 1in.

Burano. A beautifully made copy of old Venetian lace. The bars are very elaborate and the colour is ecru, which identifies it as Burano.

Machine-made copy. It feels floppy in the hand, and unlike the real thing, the stiffly beautiful point de Venise. Width 3½ins.

Brussels. This piece is real needle lace though very ugly. Width 2½ins.

Valenciennes, 1870. Border. Possibly machine-made. Width 3ins.

Valenciennes, 1870. Tie of hand-made lace. Width 6ins.

LE PUY — Bobbin Lace

Lace was made at Le Puy throughout the history of lace making. Generations of astute businessmen and women must have succeeded each other. The lace was made for the middle market. It was never a grand important lace, but a lace that ordinary men and women wore all day and every day. The directors of Le Puy were always ready to try anything to keep up sales. After complaints of difficulties in the eighteenth century during which, according to Mrs. Palliser, they were employing 100,000 people, they suffered the slump of the later part of the century. But they soon recovered and made vast quantities of lace in the nineteenth century, employing 130,000 in the mid-nineteenth century. They made lace in a wide variety of materials, silk, wool, cotton or linen and even added aloe, which was dyed black, to make a black and white lace.

Le Puy lace always copied the most expensive lace of its day. But since cheapness was the aim, it was often copied in coarse cheap thread or in an eye-catching colour. Much of it is referred to as 'peasant lace'. Cluny lace was introduced by Le Puy in the middle of the nineteenth century in an effort to break into the more expensive markets. It is an attractive geometric patterned lace that must have been a success, since one can find it easily.

Le Puy. Handmade. The pretty ground gives this lace some quality. Width 2ins.

Le Puy. Mantilla. This pretty cream piece was made to look a little like Maltese lace.

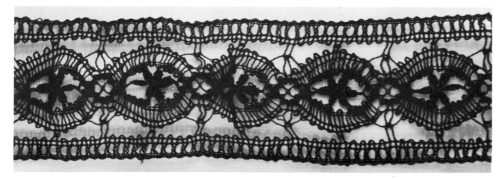

Le Puy. Following Maltese fashion, a light cheap looking lace. Width 1¾ins.

Three machine-made laces of the 1870s.

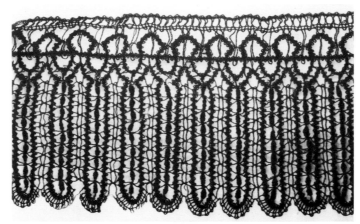

Right: Le Puy, Cluny. Width 3½ins.

Below: Chantilly. Lappet. Width 2ins.

Below right: Width 3ins.

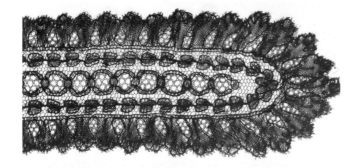

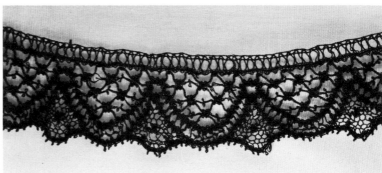

Above: Le Puy. Handmade. A graceful, balanced design which could be worn flat or gathered. Width 1¼ins.

Left: Hat veil, a half-circle of handmade lace. This is an imitation of Maltese lace, but Le Puy is much lighter in design and would have been prettier to wear.

In the 1880s, lace was not as rich or elaborate as twenty years before, but interest in old lace had grown and vast quantities of seventeenth century lace were cut up and made into contemporary garments.

One of the more curious sorts of lace appeared in the eighties. Chemical lace is made by embroidering with a machine onto a fabric. The fabric is then dissolved by dipping it into a chemical. The embroidery machine must have been difficult to manoeuvre as there are rarely any graceful lines. The result is a stiff and heavy geometric lace.

The machine lace designers continued to design the most lovely big flowers on very light graceful lace. In the house, lace was used to edge all sorts of household linens. Hand towels from Italy, made of linen, edged with lace and with six inch long fringes were always bought by visitors, carefully monogrammed and used for fifty years. They never seemed to wear out, though the fringes needed to be trimmed from time to time. In France, Mechlin and Valenciennes were copied on machines for the same purposes. Valenciennes was much used also on underclothes and children's clothes.

The Arts and Crafts movement, started by William Morris, was much admired and encouraged in the intellectual world. Towards the end of the century, it had affected design throughout the house. Furniture became simpler, rooms lighter, and the lace too became lighter and the flower designs more natural.

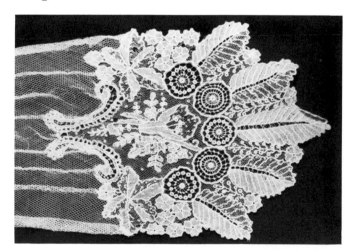

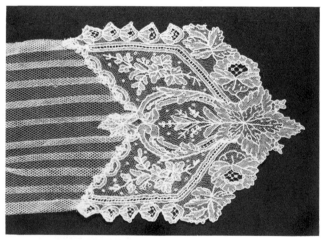

Brussels. Needle lace, worn at the ends of cravats.

Honiton or Brussels, 1890. Bobbin lace collar. Width 3ins.

Matching border. Width 3ins.

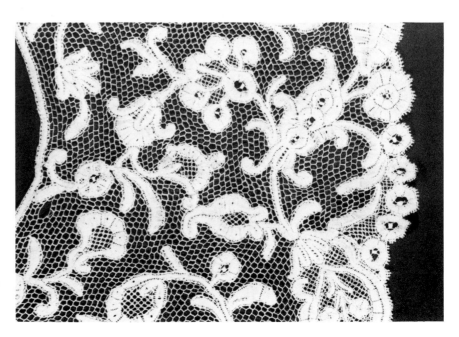

Honiton. Collar. Motifs joined by a handmade Honiton ground. Width 7½ins.

240

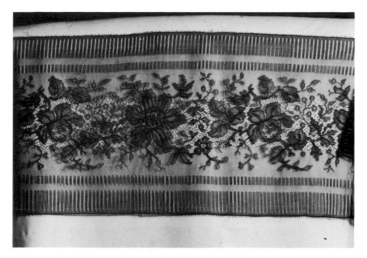

Chantilly, 1885. Machine-made. Width 10ins.

Chantilly. Machine-made. Width 40½ins.

France, 1880s. The elaborate borders gradually shrank and the flowers became bigger. This picture of a rose design shows how soft the lace was.

These elaborate orchids are not as pretty. Width 10ins.

England, 1880-90. These pictures of a handmade fichu show designs made by Walter Crane. Length 38ins., width 23ins.

France, 1880-90. This odd lace is called chemical lace. It is coarse and clumsy. Width 6ins.

France. A machine-made lace resembling Mechlin. An old design awkwardly interpreted. Width 2¼ ins.

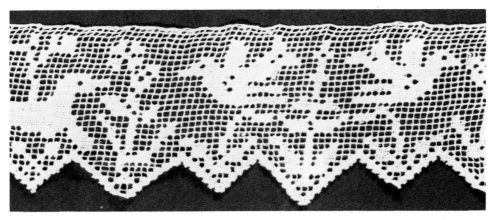

Home-made laces 1885-1900. Filet.

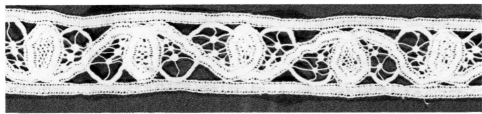

Needle lace.

Better made than most!

1890-1900

These years were remembered with nostalgia by those who knew them. Life was full of hope; standards of living were rising, trains and ships ran on schedules, and the bicycle gave freedom to many millions who had never known it before. It was sincerely believed that life was getting better and better for everyone, and would continue to do so. Women had more rights than for centuries and their masculine looking clothes showed this. Lace was limited to ties and jabots and elegant edgings and inserts on shirts and underclothes. In the house a great deal of lace was used to edge bed-linen, table linen and on mats of all sorts. The mats were to be found on dressing-tables, chests of drawers, tray-cloths and as anti-macassers. For this, lace was made in narrow widths; Valenciennes, both handmade and machine-made, was much used.

In the evenings, lace was lavishly employed in dress. In medium widths any of the white or black laces that gathered well were used on peignoirs. The wide laces with huge flowers and very wide borders were used to make dresses. Tea-gowns frothed with lace and formal dress used a great deal. The laces were mounted on colours: beige lace over pink, black lace over scarlet for instances. Rare old laces were still used for collars and berthas. These were sometimes mixed with swansdown or velvet. Lace making was still fashionable but little, if any of it, had any quality.

Handmade lace was prized for its superiority and greater cost. Or did the greater cost make it superior? There were still rich people who bought expensive lace, and there are a few handmade pieces from this period to be found.

France, 1890. This thistle design is typical of the beautiful flowered borders of this date. Cut to 7½ins.

Design of poppies. Width 8ins.

CHAPTER VIII

The Twentieth Century

The Arts and Crafts movement initiated by William Morris dominated design thought in the last quarter of the nineteenth century but had little effect on lace design. The techniques of machine lace making were so interesting that the designs became stereotyped. Design ever changing as always, moved on at the turn of the century to art nouveau. This self-conscious sinuous school of design dominated Europe until the Second World War. The flowers became bigger in the '90s, but they continued to be copies of drawings made from nature. The supporters of art nouveau wanted everything in the house to be in the exciting new style, designed to be quite different from anything seen before. The most thorough of all the shops and galleries catering to this new taste was the Wiener Werkstatte at Vienna.

By 1900 the impetus from the Arts and Crafts movement had petered out. Technologically the new century had everything to look forward to; politically Europe was uneasy. The art nouveau movement was developed by a group of great designers. It took slightly different paths in different countries, but everywhere it was new.

The Wiener Werkstatte at Vienna was founded in 1903 by Joseph Hoffman and other artists and designers. There they designed everything needed for the house, including furniture, cutlery, textiles, tiles and decorations. One house was built and furnished completely. The contents of this house have recently been bought by the Felton Bequest for the

Vienna, 1910. Typical traditional lace of the period. Cloths like these would have been found in most houses.
Private Collection.

Museum at Melbourne. The lace made for the Wiener Werkstatte was made primarily for table and household use. The beautiful flower shaped mats with their sparse and delicate decorations are in sharp contrast to the traditional lace from the same private collection. The latter is also pretty, but does not have the impact of the art nouveau designed pieces. When the Wiener Werkstatte closed in 1932, it was presumably the victim of the depression of the 1930s; but lifestyles too had changed and it is always difficult to keep the impetus going in design.

Table-cloths of the same date as the preceding illustrations. The difference in design is overwhelming. They were designed by Dagobert Peche, d. 1923, who designed textiles and silver for the Wiener Werkstatte.
Private Collection.

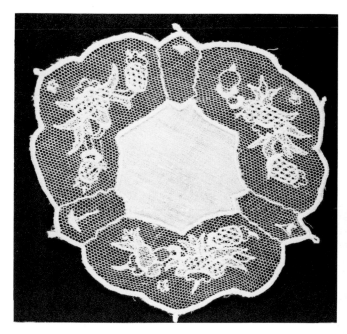

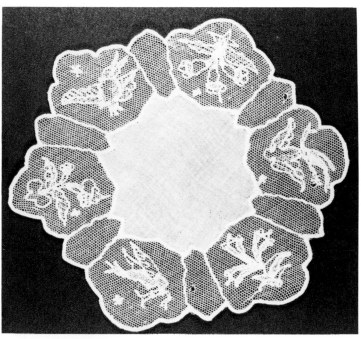

Table mats from three different sets. Also designed for the Wiener Werkstatte.
Private Collection.

Italy, 1922. This handsome piece of lace was made under orders from the Ars Aemilia, the charity needlework service founded in Bologna. Well made, it is presumably a copy of a museum piece. Width 2¼ ins.

Brussels, 1910. A beautiful handmade lace with a kat ground, an art nouveau design worked in the Brussels tradition.

Mechlin, 1935-45. Handkerchief. 12ins. square with 1¼ins. border.

The so-called monkey design. Its real name is 'aape', hence the odd English name. It is taught today as an early lesson in the making of Flemish lace. A traditional design to contrast with the modern lace that follows.

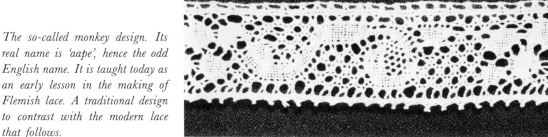

Dragonfly, designed and made by Ann Collier. 6ins. by 8ins.

These pieces worked in bobbin lace by Ann Collier show a really modern approach to the use of traditional techniques.

Needle lace ship design by Ann Collier.

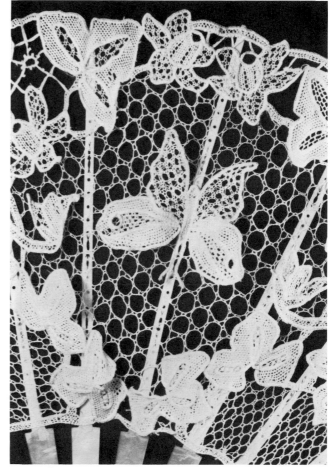

Fan, elegantly covered with flowers and butterflies in a variety of stitches, also by Ann Collier.

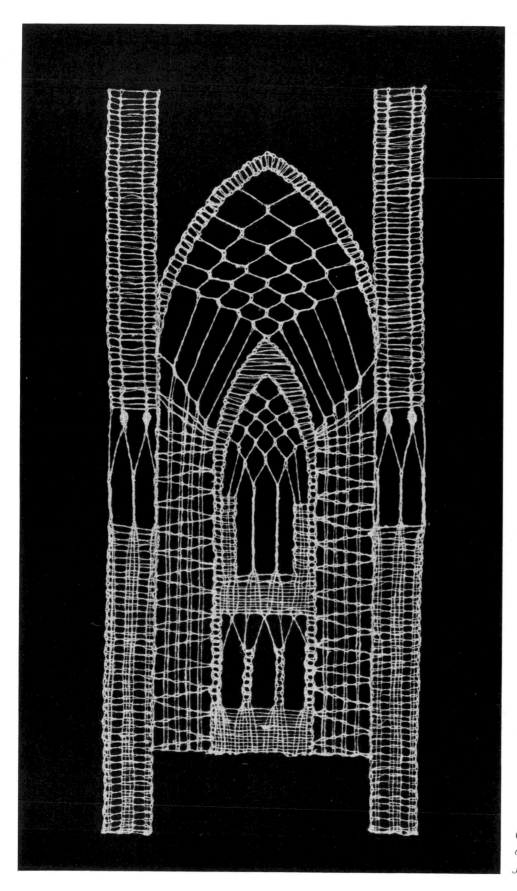

Czechoslovakia. 'Gothic Prague', designed and made by Marie Jarkouska. 14ins. by 6ins.

Czechoslovakia. Detail from a long piece illustrating a village wedding, designed and made by B. Hanujova.

Butterfly, copyright Mo Gibbs, designed and made by her.

Designed and made by S.C. Straughair and published with her permission. Copyright of The Lace Guild.

1980. Designed and made by Isobel Rendell. Photograph, Yukio Wakasugi. Copyright of The Lace Guild.

Detail.

Select Bibliography

There are many books about lace, but they all derive from the book by Mrs. Bury Palliser, first published in 1865. Mrs. Palliser studied lace seriously; she traced its history and travelled all over Europe, checking on every fact. Her point of view was of course different from ours today, but we must be grateful to her for learning so much and passing it on to us. A full list of books would not be of much use; most of the old books are out of print and unavailable. The following books are recommended and generally available:

Earnshaw, Pat. *The Identification of Lace.* Shire Publications, 1980.

Earnshaw, Pat. *Bobbin and Needle Laces.* Batsford, London, 1983.

Jourdain, M. *Old Lace.* Batsford, London, 1908.

Lefebure, Ernest. *Embroidery and Lace.* H. Grevel and Co., London, 1888.

Levey, Santina. *Lace, A History.* Victoria and Albert Museum, London, 1983.

Longfield, Ada. *Irish Lace.* Eason and Son Ltd., Dublin, 1978.

Palliser, Mrs. Bury. *History of Lace.* Ed. Margaret Jourdain, Sampson, Low and Co. Ltd., London, 1902.

Simeon, Margaret. *The History of Lace.* Stainer and Bell, London, 1979.

Wardle, Patricia. *Victorian Lace.* Herbert Jenkins, London, 1968.

Glossary

anti-macassar	A nineteenth century decorated rectangle of white linen used on the backs of chairs to protect the upholstery from macassar oil used by men on their hair.
applied lace	Needle or bobbin lace motifs sewn onto a ground of machine net or handmade mesh. Sometimes called application lace.
bars	Also called brides. These are the links that connect motifs in needle lace. They were also made in bobbin lace when needle lace was being copied. Under a magnifying glass it is easy to see the difference between a buttonholed needle lace bar and a plaited bobbin bar.
bertha	A collar made by gathering a very wide border of lace onto a boat neckline.
bone lace	English name for bobbin lace, as bones were used in the making.
brides tortillées	Bars whipped, not buttonholed, as in early Argentan.
cap back	A specially shaped piece of lace made to fit the back of the head. The rest of the cap was made in different shapes according to fashion.
continuous lace	A name for straight lace.
cordonnet	A heavy edge to a motif. As they were made in different ways in different laces, they are one way of identifying a piece of lace.
ecru	A light brown colour much admired in the nineteenth and early twentieth centuries. Either the thread was dyed or the lace was boiled in tea or coffee.
engageants	French name for shaped cuffs used during the seventeenth and eighteenth centuries.
fichu	A square which was folded or shaped to make a full collar.
filling stitches	Decorative stitches used in the middle of motifs.
fontange	The high looped head-dress worn at the end of the seventeenth century.
footing	A narrow looped strip, machine-made, sewn along the bottom of machine-made lace to make it look hand-made, or onto the bottom of handmade lace to conceal damage to the edge.
ground	The net or mesh which joins motifs, helpful in identifying the origin and date of lace.

half stitch	A bobbin lace stitch which looks diagonal.
heading	The narrow strip of lace or braid sewn onto the top of a piece of lace to prevent wear.
jabot	A straight length of cloth put once or twice around the neck, with an elaborate decorated knot or fall at the front.
lappets	Worn as a pair, one on each side of the head, hanging from a cap. Square ends were made from the late seventeenth century; slightly rounded ends from the early eighteenth century. By 1720 lappets had rounded ends and shaped sides. They were also worn between 1825 and 1875.
macramé	The elaborate knotting of lace and fringes.
mixed lace	Lace which is made with both needles and bobbin, and sometimes machine lace and net.
motif	The units of design linked by bars or ground.
net	Machine-made ground, first produced in 1763. The early forms are difficult to distinguish from handmade grounds. In 1809, Heathcoat invented a machine which makes a net with a mesh that looks like Lille ground.
non-continuous lace	Lace in which threads are added or taken away as necessary to the design.
picot	A knot used to decorate bars.
point de raccroc	An invisible stitch joining the strips which make up a ground, the stitch varying according to the type of lace.
point plat	French name for flat lace, made mainly in Venice.
points d'esprit	Small squares of solid thread scattered in a pattern over the ground or in the motif.
raised work	Any work added to the top of needle or bobbin lace which gives a third dimension.
re-ground	To replace a ground, often done at Burano in the late nineteenth century. Sometimes done to make a lace look more valuable.
reseau	French for ground.
ruedas	A round lace invented in Spain and much used in South America.
straight lace	Bobbin lace made with the same number of threads from start to finish.
toile	The solid pieces of a design motif. In needle lace the toile is made in buttonhole stitch; in bobbin lace it is woven; in the finest lace it looks like lawn.
trolley	The name for different kinds of simple lace made at various times in England.
whole stitch	Used in bobbin lace, it looks like plain weaving.

Index

Notes: In order to facilitate the use of this index we have entered laces under appropriate place names. Stitches are listed individually. Page numbers printed in italics refer to illustrations.